BACKSTI

Competitive

Swimming Drills

Over 65 BACKSTROKE Drills
Improve Technique | Add Variety
For Coaches | For Teachers | For Swimmers

Second edition published in the United Kingdom 2020
Copyright © Eatsleepswimcoach

https://eatsleepswimcoach.com

Contents

Welcome

A very warm welcome to 'Backstroke Competitive Swimming Drills'.

About this publication

This publication provides coaches, teachers and swimmers with a series of tried and tested competitive backstroke swimming drills.

● These drills can be used to develop and maintain a particular or range of backstroke skill/s.

● They can be easily incorporated and adapted into your training or teaching programme, whether you coach or teach rookie or national swimmers.

Delivering the technical demands of our sport

Competitive swimming can be a gruelling sport, requiring swimmers to undertake many hours of repetitive training each week, in pursuit of excellence.

● Developing a training or teaching programme that delivers the technical demands of our sport, while at the same time adding variety to your sessions can be an ongoing process.

● This can be both difficult and time-consuming to achieve.

● Training or teaching programmes without fresh stimuli are in real danger of demotivating swimmers, coaches and teachers alike.

● Over the past twenty-five plus years as a head coach, coach and teacher, I have managed to collate a large portfolio of competitive backstroke drills.

● I have used these to develop many young competitive backstroke swimmers from club to county, regional/state and national levels, the best of which are published here.

Publication focus

This publication focuses on the stroke's key technical areas.

● Each has its own dedicated chapter, breaking down the stroke into its key constituent parts, to help both the coach, the teacher and the swimmer develop and maintain a great backstroke.

About Us - EatSleepSwimCoach

EatSleepSwimCoach is a competitive swimming website.

● Our team includes swimmers, swimming parents, teachers and coaches.

● With over 50 years of combined competitive swimming experience, both in the pool and open water.

● We provide swimming advice, drills, exercises, hacks, insight and tips.

● We produce publications, posts, articles and digital downloads on a wide range of swimming subjects.

● These include stroke technique, training drills and how to optimise training and competitive performance.

For further information please visit our website by using the following link: https://eatsleepswimcoach.com/

Facebook Group

EatSleepSwimCoach administers the **Competitive Swimming Exchange** Facebook Group.

● This is a competitive swimming group to help exchange ideas and information to collectively improve the sport we love.

● It's an international group for all swimmers, coaches, teachers, masters, triathletes and swimming parents.

● In fact, it's for all those who are interested in competitive swimming, either in the pool or in open water.

For further information about joining this group please use the following   link: https://www.facebook.com/groups/thecompetitiveswimmingexchange

Coaching & Teaching an Introduction

Competitive swimming training

Competitive swimming training requires the swimmer to perform repetitive technical and physical drills, to master a set of key skills.

● This enables them to perform to the best of their ability, when under the pressure of competition.

● Repetitive training enables the swimmer to adapt their training to their 'muscle memory'*, enabling them to automatically perform as taught during competition.

(*muscle memory - the ability to reproduce a movement without conscious thought, acquired as a result of frequent repetition of that movement)

● If the training is repetitively performed with a perfect technique, then the muscle memory will store this perfect technique.

● However, if the training is repetitively performed with a poor technique, then the muscle memory will store this poor technique.

● Once a poor technique has been stored, this can be very difficult to correct.

● For any coach or teacher, it is important that they 'consistently and persistently' incorporate perfectly performed drills into their training or teaching programmes to reinforce and develop a great butterfly technique.

Swimming drills

I introduce drills into every training session.

- I incorporate them into every warm-up routine.
- I also conduct a twenty-minute 'drills based' activity after the warm-up, before the swimmers become fatigued.
- I have found this is long enough to teach drills correctly and short enough for swimmers to maintain focus.

Make progress slowly

I have found that it pays to be patient when introducing a new drill.
- Some swimmers quickly learn some techniques and struggle to learn others.
- Coaches and teachers should use multiple coaching and teaching formats.
- Some swimmers may prefer to learn via verbal or written communication.
- Other swimmers may prefer to learn via a physical demonstration.
- Wherever possible, I use swimmers who have mastered a technique to demonstrate specific drills.
- I have found that using a senior swimmer to demonstrate drills to junior swimmers, is a very effective way of getting my coaching points across.

I have found the use of fins very useful while introducing some of these drills to younger or less experienced swimmers.
- It can help them to increase their speed and power and can also help to increase the swimmer's confidence and help reduce the chance of them becoming fatigued.

Only once a good technique has been mastered should the level of difficulty be gradually increased.
- These drills can be adapted and developed accordingly, by increasing the distance, intensity or decreasing the target time.

Training aids

Resistance, assistance and variety can also be added by the introduction of training aids such as:
- Bungee cords
- Drag belts/shorts
- Hand paddles
- Kickboards
- Pull buoys
- Snorkels

- Swim fins

Safety First
- Always ensure the safety of the swimmers in your charge, whilst carrying out any drill.
- Whether starting in the water or from a dive, please ensure your swimmers have enough room to allow the correct and unhurried execution of the drill.
- When starting any drill that requires a dive, please ensure the swimmer can perform a racing dive safely and they have achieved the relevant competitive start accreditation.

Please note the drills contained in this publication are performed in a 25m pool.
- Please make the relevant adjustments if you coach or teach in a pool of a different distance.

I hope you find this publication useful, enjoy your coaching and teaching.

Coach Arthur

Chapter 1: Backstroke an Introduction

Backstroke is the stroke many swimmers start to perform first.
● This is often because backstroke has the advantage of easier 'face out of the water' breathing.
● However, backstroke has the disadvantage in that the swimmer cannot see where they are going.

Since backstroke is performed on their back, the swimmer cannot engage as many of the body's larger muscle groups as they can while swimming freestyle or butterfly.
● To compensate for this, backstroke should be performed with a high stroke rate, assisted by the rotation of the swimmer's body, especially their shoulders, trunk and hips.

The competitive start in backstroke is unique in the fact that it starts in the water.
● The current law allows backstroke swimmers to kick underwater for 15m at the start and at the turn at the end of each length/lap.
● This requires backstroke swimmers to have an efficient, fast and powerful underwater dolphin kick.

Backstroke can be performed as an alternative warm-up and cool-down stroke to freestyle.
● It can also be used as a recovery stroke for freestyle swimmers complaining of sore or aching shoulders.

The correct position for an effective backstroke

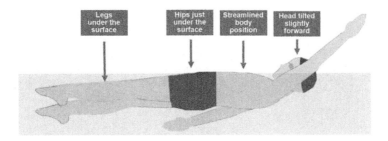

Body position
• The swimmer's body should be horizontal, supine and streamlined.
• The swimmer should ensure that they engage their core to help ensure they do not arch their back, to help ensure that their hips and shoulders will not sink too much.

Head position
• The head should be tilted slightly forward, like resting on a pillow, to help ensure their hips and legs remain under the surface.
• This should also help to ensure that the swimmer's back will not be arched, and their hips and shoulders will not sink too much.
• The swimmer should ensure that their head is not too high out of the water, which could create added resistance.
• They should ensure that the level of the water covers the swimmer's ears.

Hips position
• The hips should be just under the surface of the water to ensure the legs also remain under the surface.

Leg position
• The swimmer's leg should be close together and under the surface of the water.

Feet position
• Feet should be in a pointed (plantar flexion) position, which reduces drag and places the feet in the optimum position for maximum propulsion.

Chapter 2: The Body & Head Position

Introduction: The correct body and head position are extremely important in the development of an efficient competitive backstroke technique.
• It helps to reduce drag and establishes the correct platform from which an effective arm stroke and leg kick can be performed.

The key components for an effective body and head position
• The swimmer's body should be horizontal, supine and streamlined.
• They should ensure that they engage their core to ensure they do not arch their back, to ensure their hips and shoulders will not sink too much.
• Their head should be tilted slightly forward, like resting on a pillow.
• This should help to ensure that the swimmer's back will not be arched and that their hips will not sink too much.
• The swimmer should ensure that their head is not too high out of the water, which could create added resistance.
• The level of the water should cover the swimmer's ears.

2.1: Kicking with a kickboard overhead

Purpose: This is an introductory drill to help to develop the swimmer's body position.

How to perform this drill: The swimmer should start this drill from a push & glide in a horizontal streamlined supine (on their back) position.

- They should hold a kickboard in both hands and place the kickboard above their head, with their arms outstretched.
- They should hold the bottom edge of the kickboard and perform a steady flutter (backstroke) kick.
- Their head should be tilted slightly forward, like resting on a pillow.
- This should help to ensure that the swimmer's back will not be arched, and their hips will not sink too much.
- The swimmer should ensure that their head is not too high out of the water, which could create added resistance.
- The level of the water should cover the swimmer's ears.
- They should complete this drill for one length/lap of the pool (25m)

Coaching points: While performing this drill, the swimmer should ensure that they engage their core to help ensure that they do not arch their back.

*How to engage your core

Engaging your core muscles ensures they are correctly aligned, to help support and perform certain swimming drills and skills effectively.

- To engage their core, the swimmer should continue to breathe normally.
- They should then tighten/contract their stomach muscles while drawing their navel towards their spine.

Core strength development

To effectively engage their core, the swimmer should develop their core strength.

- The swimmer should perform core development training exercises such as crunches and planks as a regular part of their dryland/land training programme.

2.2: Cup balance

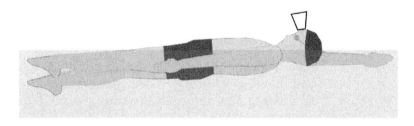

Purpose: This is a great exercise to help the swimmer develop the correct backstroke head position.

How to perform this drill: The swimmer should start this drill by half filling a paper cup (with a flat bottom) with pool water.

- They should then perform this drill from a push & glide in a horizontal streamlined supine (on their back) position, whilst still holding the cup.
- The swimmer then proceeds by balancing the cup on their forehead, trying to ensure that it doesn't fall into the water.
- Their head should be tilted slightly forward, like resting on a pillow.
- This should help to ensure that the swimmer's back will not be arched, and their hips will not sink too much.
- The swimmer should ensure that their head is not too high out of the water, which will create added resistance.
- The level of the water should cover the swimmer's ears.
- If the cup does fall, then the swimmer should place the cup back onto their head and proceed with the drill.
- Once mastered, the swimmer should attempt to swim full stroke backstroke for a length/lap of the pool, without the cup falling.

Coaching points: This drill requires the swimmer to intensely focus on their head position.

Chapter 3: Body Rotation

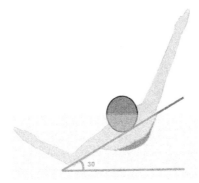

Introduction: The main propulsion for an effective backstroke comes from the swimmer's arm stroke.

● Since backstroke is performed on their back, the swimmer cannot engage as many of the body's larger muscle groups as they can while performing either freestyle or butterfly.

● To help to engage as many of these muscles as possible, the swimmer should perform a smooth rotation of their body, especially their shoulders, trunk and hips.

● Backstroke should also be performed with a high stroke rate.

● Coaches may wish to allow younger or inexperienced swimmers the use of fins while they master these drills.

The key components for an effective body rotation

● The swimmer should ensure they perform a controlled and smooth rotation of their shoulders, trunk and hips.

● The swimmer should ensure that they do not rotate their body too much, as this could result in a too deeper arm pull, which could slow their stroke rate.

● They should not rotate their shoulders, trunk and hips at more than approximately thirty degrees.

3.1: Hands in pockets

Purpose: This is an introductory drill to help develop the swimmer's shoulder, trunk and hip rotation skills.

● Which should help to facilitate a more powerful and effective arm pulling action.

How to perform this drill: The swimmer should start this drill from a push & glide in a horizontal streamlined supine (on their back) position, while performing a steady flutter kick.

● The swimmer should place both of their arms down by their sides ('hands in pockets').

● Whilst continuing to perform a steady flutter kick, the swimmer should slowly and smoothly, rotate their shoulders, trunk and hips to an approximate thirty degrees angle, on their right-hand side.

● The swimmer should then perform six flutter kicks, then they should slowly and smoothly, rotate their shoulders, trunk and hips to an approximate thirty degrees angle, on their left-hand side.

● The swimmer should then perform six flutter kicks, and smoothly, rotate back onto the right-hand side.

● They should continue to repeat this drill for one length/lap of the pool (25m)

● Younger or less experienced swimmers may find the use of fins useful while learning this drill.

Coaching points: Once mastered, the swimmer can slowly increase the speed of their smooth shoulder, trunk and hip rotations.

3.2: Extended rotation

Purpose: This drill helps to further develop the swimmer's shoulder, trunk and hip rotation skills.

How to perform this drill: The swimmer should start this drill from a push & glide in a horizontal streamlined supine (on their back) position, while performing a steady flutter kick.

● They should place their left arm by their side.

● They should place their right arm into a fully extended position above their head.

● The swimmer should then rotate their shoulders and hips on to their right-hand side, with the extended arm, at an approximate thirty degrees angle.

- They should perform six flutter kicks, holding that position.
- The swimmer should then slowly and smoothly, rotate their shoulders and hips on to their left-hand side, at an approximate thirty degrees angle.
- While they place their right arm by their side and place their left arm into a fully extended position above their head.
- They should then perform six flutter kicks, holding that position.
- The swimmer should continue this drill alternating sides, for one length/lap of the pool.
- Once mastered, the swimmer can slowly increase the speed of their smooth shoulder and hip rotations.

Chapter 4: Sculling

Introduction: Sculling is an often-overlooked key set of swimming skills.
- Efficient sculling can give the swimmer 'a feel for the water'.
- It can help them place their hands in the correct position, to help them to gain maximum propulsion during the completion of the arm stroke.
- Sculling can be great drills to introduce during a cool-down or recovery swim.

The sculling hand position
- The swimmer's fingers should be slightly apart, and the hands should be slightly cupped.

To obtain the correct hand position for sculling
- The swimmer should place their hands on the cheeks of their face, ensuring that their fingers are very slightly apart.
- They should then remove their hands from their face, whilst keeping their fingers slightly apart.
- Their hands should now be in the optimum position for effective sculling.

4.1: Double arm mid-point scull

Purpose: This drill introduces the swimmer to the sculling action required for the mid-point of the backstroke arm stroke.
• Which should start from level with the top of the swimmer's shoulders, down to their hips.
How to perform this drill: The swimmer should start this drill from a push & glide in a horizontal supine (on their back) position.
• The swimmer should scull headfirst.
• The swimmer's feet should be in a pointed plantar flexion position.
• The swimmer's arms should be outstretched, perpendicular to their body (90 degrees) level with the top of their shoulders, with a slight bend at the elbow.
• They should commence this drill with a 'thumbs up' double bent arm sculling action, starting level with their shoulders and finishing at the hips.
• The swimmer should recover their hands underwater, horizontal to the surface, by turning the palm of their hands to face the bottom of the pool.
• They should complete this drill for one length/lap of the pool (25m).
• Younger or less experienced swimmers can perform a minimal flutter kick, to help ensure that they keep their legs in a streamlined position.

4.2: Single arm mid-point scull

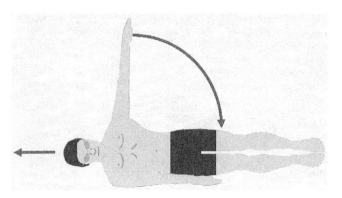

Purpose: This drill helps to further develop the swimmer's sculling action required for the mid-point of the full backstroke stroke while incorporating a smooth shoulder and hip rotation.

How to perform this drill: The swimmer should start this drill from a push & glide in a horizontal supine (on their back) position.

• They should ensure that they have their hands by their side.

• The swimmer should scull headfirst.

• The swimmer's feet should be in a pointed plantar flexion position.

• The swimmer should then slowly and smoothly, rotate their shoulders, trunk and hips on to their right side, at an approximate thirty degrees angle.

• The swimmer should then extend their right arm out perpendicular (at right angles) to the top of their shoulder just below the surface of the water.

• They should then start to perform a 'thumbs up' single arm sculling action, while gradually increasing the bend in the arm to 90 degrees.

• The sculling action should start level with the shoulder and finish at their hips.

• The swimmer should recover the hands underwater, horizontal to the surface, by turning the palm of their hands to face the bottom of the pool.

• They should complete this drill for one length/lap of the pool (25m).

• The swimmer should then repeat this drill using their left hand.

• Younger or less experienced swimmers can perform a minimal flutter kick, to help ensure that they keep their legs in a streamlined position.

4.3: Double arm backend scull

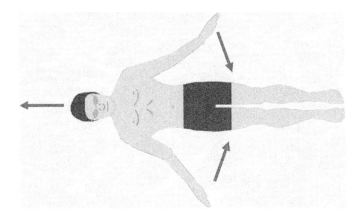

Purpose: This drill helps to further develop the swimmer's sculling action required for the backend of the full backstroke stroke.

● This drill should start with the swimmer's hands level with the swimmer's hips and finish with their arms fully extended, with their palms resting against their thighs.

How to perform this drill: The swimmer should start this drill from a push & glide in a horizontal supine (on their back) position.

● The swimmer should scull headfirst.

● The swimmer's feet should be in a pointed plantar flexion position.

● The swimmer should have both hands starting level with their hips.

● They should perform a sculling action by 'pushing' the water towards their feet until both arms are fully extended, with the palms resting against their thighs, in a thumbs-up position.

● The swimmer should recover their hands underwater, horizontal to the surface, by turning the palm of their hands to face the bottom of the pool.

● They should complete this drill for one length/lap of the pool (25m).

● Younger or less experienced swimmers can perform a minimal flutter kick, to help ensure that they keep their legs in a streamlined position.

.

Chapter 5: The Arm Stroke

Introduction: The main propulsive force in backstroke comes from the arm stroke, which is aided by a smooth rotation of the swimmer's body, primarily the shoulders, trunk and hips.

The key components for an effective arm pull

The recovery phase
- The swimmer's hand should exit the water fully extended and thumb first.
- Their arm should be assisted out of the water by the rotation of their body.
- The swimmer's arm should be fully extended and brush past their ear, before entering the water.

The entry phase
- The swimmer's hand should enter the water fully extended with their little finger first.
- They should ensure that they do not start to pull as soon as their hand enters the water, as this can cause additional drag.
- To further reduce drag, as soon as their hand enters the water, they should turn the back of their hand to face the bottom of the pool.

The catch phase
- As a part of a continuous action, the swimmer should scull with a bent elbow with their hand outwards and downwards, until it reaches a position in a line between their upper chest and shoulders.

• The swimmer should then rotate their hand to ninety degrees, so their thumb is facing up towards the pool surface and their little finger is facing down towards the bottom of the pool.

The finishing phase
• The swimmer should then push their hand through the water until their arm is fully flexed by their thigh.
• The swimmer's hand should exit the water fully extended and thumb first.

5.1: Double arm pull

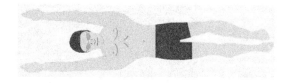

Purpose: This is an excellent introductory drill for developing the swimmer's backstroke arm pull, by focusing on their arm and hand positions.

How to perform this drill: The swimmer should start this drill from a push & glide in a horizontal streamlined supine (on their back) position, while performing a steady flutter kick.
• They should then proceed to perform a double arm pull.
• The swimmer's arms should be fully extended and brush past their ears before entering the water between the line of the shoulder and the centre line of the head.
• The swimmer's hands should enter with their little fingers first.
• They should ensure that they do not start to pull as soon as their hand enters the water, as this can cause additional drag.
• As soon as their hand enters the water, the swimmer should turn the back of their hand facing the bottom of the pool.
• Then as part of a continuous action, the swimmer should scull with a bent elbow and their hand outwards and downwards until it reaches a position in a line between their upper chest and shoulders.
• The swimmer should then rotate their hand at ninety degrees, so their thumb is facing up towards the pool surface and their little finger is facing down towards the bottom of the pool.
• They should then push their hand through the water until their arm is fully extended by their thigh.
• Their hand should exit the water thumb first.

- The swimmer should ensure that the arms finish the recovery with both arms fully extended.
- They should complete this drill for one length/lap of the pool (25m).

5.2: Start/stop drill

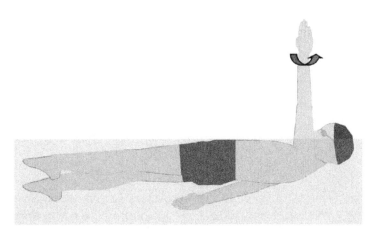

Purpose: This is an excellent drill for developing the swimmer's 'little finger' first, hand entry.

How to perform this drill: The swimmer should start this drill from a push & glide in a horizontal streamlined supine (on their back) position.

- They should proceed to perform a full backstroke stroke.
- They should ensure that their hand exits the stroke thumb first.
- As the swimmer recovers their arm, they should fully extend it vertically.
- The swimmer should then pause their stroke with their arm in a vertical position.
- The pause should be just long enough for the swimmer to turn their hand to a little finger first entry position.
- They then proceed to enter this hand into the water to continue their stroke.
- The swimmer should continue this drill using alternating arms for one length/lap of the pool.

5.3: Single-arm pull

Purpose: This drill helps to further develop the swimmer's arm pulling and body rotation skills.

How to perform this drill: The swimmer should start this drill from a push & glide in a horizontal streamlined supine (on their back) position, while performing a steady flutter kick.

• They should fully extend their right arm above their head while placing their left hand by their side.

• The swimmer should then proceed to perform a series of single-arm pulls with their right arm.

• They should ensure that they smoothly rotate their shoulders and hips on to their right-hand side, at an approximate thirty degrees angle, during every single arm pull.

• They should complete this drill for one length/lap of the pool (25m).

• The swimmer should repeat this drill performing left arm single arm pulls.

Variations: Younger or inexperienced swimmers may find this drill easier by holding a kickboard with their non-pulling arm to their chest or using fins.

5.4: Single arm pull 3/3

Purpose: This drill helps to further develop the swimmer's pulling and body rotation skills.

How to perform this drill: The swimmer should start this drill from a push & glide in a horizontal streamlined supine (on their back) position, while performing a steady flutter kick.

• They should fully extend their right arm above their head while placing their left hand by their side.

• The swimmer should ensure that they smoothly rotate their body on to their right side, at an approximate thirty degrees angle.

• The swimmer should then proceed to perform three single-arm pulls with their right arm.

• The swimmer should then slowly and smoothly, rotates their body on to their left side, at an approximate thirty degrees angle.

• They should fully extend their left arm above their head while placing their right hand by their side.

• The swimmer should then proceed to perform three single-arm pulls with their left arm.

• They should complete this drill alternating arms, for one length/lap of the pool (25m).

5.5: Catch-up

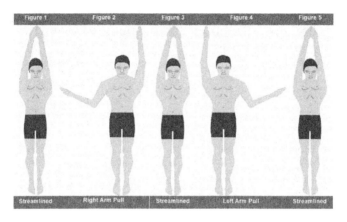

Purpose: This is a classic drill to further develop the swimmer's arm pulling and body rotation skills.

How to perform this drill: The swimmer should start this drill from a push & glide in a horizontal streamlined supine (on their back) position, while performing a steady flutter kick.

• They should fully extend both arms above their head in a streamlined position (figure 1).

• The swimmer should then slowly and smoothly, rotate their body on to their right-hand side, at an approximate thirty degrees angle.

• Then they perform a single arm pull with their right arm (figure 2).

• The swimmer should ensure that their right arm finishes the stroke back into a fully extended streamlined position (figure 3).

• Once the swimmer's right arm has 'caught up' with and is alongside their fully extended left arm.

• The swimmer should then rotate their body on to their left-hand side, at an approximate thirty degrees angle and perform a single-arm pull with their left arm (figure 4).

● The swimmer should ensure that their left arm finishes the stroke back into a fully extended streamlined position (figure 5).

● They should repeat this drill for one length/lap of the pool (25m).

5.6: Pull with a pull buoy

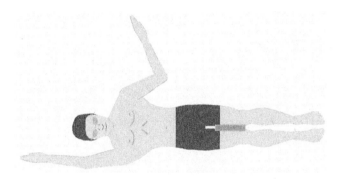

Purpose: This drill helps to develop the swimmer's arm pull, by isolating the arm stroke and increasing resistance, essential for an effective backstroke.

How to perform this drill: The swimmer should start this drill from a push & glide in a horizontal streamlined supine (on their back) position, with a pull buoy placed between their upper thighs.

● The swimmer should then perform alternate full arm strokes, while the legs are immobilised by the pull buoy.

● Although pull buoys can restrict body and hip rotation, the swimmer should still focus on achieving a smooth body rotation.

● The swimmer should focus on ensuring that their arms finish their recovery with them fully extended.

● They should ensure that their little finger enters the water first on each arm pull.

● This drill can be conducted over repeat sets of 100m/200m.

● I prefer, conducting a 'pyramid' in 100m steps.

● For example, 100m, 200m, 300m, 400m, 300m, 200m, 100m (steps of 50m for younger swimmers).

Variations: To further increase resistance and work their core the swimmer should place the pull buoy between their ankles.

● Another variation is to use a kickboard instead of a pull buoy.

● This can help to further engage the core body muscles by making the swimmer tighten their stomach, thigh and buttock muscles to keep the kick board in place.

5.7: Pulling with fists and open hands

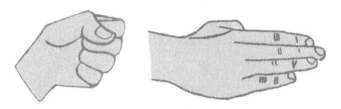

Purpose: This arm pulling drill can help develop the swimmer's 'feel for the water' by the introduction of alternate clenched fists and open hands swimming.

How to perform this drill: The swimmer should start this drill from a push and glide from the end of the pool in a horizontal supine streamlined position, with clenched fists.

• The swimmer should proceed to swim six arm strokes with clenched fists.

• They should then proceed to perform the next six strokes with normal open hands.

• The swimmer should focus on ensuring that their arms finish their recovery with them fully extended.

• They should ensure that their little finger enters the water first on each open hand pull.

• Their feet should be in a pointed (plantar flexion) position.

• They should complete this drill for one length/lap of the pool (25m)

• This drill can be performed with or without a pull buoy.

5.8: Pulling with streamlined legs

Purpose: This arm pulling drill, without a pull buoy combines arm pulling and core strength development.

How to perform this drill: The swimmer should start this drill from a push & glide at the end of the pool, in a streamlined horizontal and supine position (on their back).

• They should focus on keeping their legs motionless and in a

streamlined position throughout this drill, without allowing their legs to drop.
- The swimmer should still focus on achieving a smooth body rotation.
- They should also focus on ensuring that their arms finish their recovery with them fully extended.
- They should ensure that their little finger enters the water first on each arm pull.
- The swimmer should engage their core while performing this drill*.
- Their feet should be in a pointed (plantar flexion) position.
- They should complete this drill for one length/lap of the pool (25m)

Variation: Some coaches prefer their swimmers to perform this drill using an ankle strap/band.
- These are placed over their ankles to help eliminate kicking when pulling.

5.9: Pulling with crossed legs

Purpose: A further arm pulling drill, without a pull buoy which combines arm pulling and core strength development.

How to perform this drill: The swimmer should start this drill from a push & glide at the end of the pool, in a streamlined horizontal and supine position (on their back), while keeping their legs crossed.
- They should focus on keeping their legs motionless and in a streamlined position, throughout this drill, without allowing their legs to drop.
- The swimmer should engage their core while performing this drill*.
- The swimmer should still focus on achieving a smooth body rotation.
- They should focus on ensuring that their arms finish their recovery with them fully extended.
- They should ensure that their little finger enters the water first on each arm pull.
- Their feet should be in a pointed (plantar flexion) position.
- They should complete this drill for one length/lap of the pool (25m)

*How to engage your core

Engaging your core muscles ensures they are correctly aligned, to help support and perform certain swimming drills and skills effectively.

● To engage their core, the swimmer should continue to breathe normally.

● They should then tighten/contract their stomach muscles while drawing their navel towards their spine.

Core strength development

To effectively engage their core, the swimmer should develop their core strength.

● The swimmer should perform core development training exercises such as crunches and planks as a regular part of their dryland/land training programme.

Chapter 6: Stroke Counting

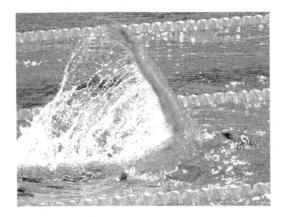

Introduction: Stroke counting is a key swimming skill, which helps the swimmer develop and maintain a long, controlled, consistent and effective arm stroke.

● Stroke counting involves the swimmer counting the number of strokes (each time each hand enters the water) that they take to complete a given distance.

● Please note there is no one correct stroke count total, as swimmers are all shapes, sizes, abilities and strengths.

● Therefore, the number of strokes it takes to complete a certain distance can be different for each swimmer.

6.1: Establishing stroke count

Purpose: This is the first in a series of stroke count drills, which introduces the swimmer to establishing a stroke count.

How to perform this drill: The swimmer should start this drill from a push & glide from the wall at the end of the pool in a supine (on their back) streamlined position.

● They should then proceed by performing a full stroke backstroke for one length/lap of the pool at a steady pace, with great technique.

● The swimmer should count the number of strokes (each time each hand enters the water) that they take to complete a length/lap of the

25

pool.

• When they have finished this drill, it's important to ensure that they allow the swimmers swimming behind them enough room to allow them to complete this drill.

6.2: Reducing stroke count

Purpose: This is the second in the series of stroke count drills, which introduces the swimmer to reducing their stroke count.

How to perform this drill: The swimmer should start this drill from a push & glide from the wall at the end of the pool in a supine (on their back) streamlined position.

• They should then proceed by performing full stroke backstroke for one length/lap of the pool at a steady pace, with great technique.

• They should reduce their stroke count by stronger kicking, stronger arm pulls, better underwater kicking from the start, a better technical stroke or a combination of all of these.

• When they have finished this drill, it's important to ensure that they allow the swimmers swimming behind them enough room to allow them to complete this drill.

6.3: Holding stroke count

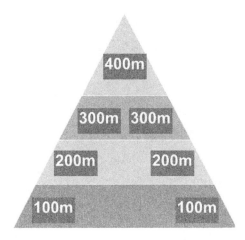

Purpose: This is the third in a series of stroke count drills, which introduces the swimmer to holding their stroke count over a longer distance.

How to perform this drill: Once a regular stroke count has been established.

● The next stage is for the swimmer to 'hold' (maintain) their regular stroke count over a longer distance.

● This drill can be conducted over repeat sets of 100m/200m.

● I prefer, conducting a 'pyramid' in 100m steps.

● For example, 100m, 200m, 300m, 400m, 300m, 200m, 100m (steps of 50m for younger swimmers).

● The swimmer should start this drill from a push & glide from the wall at the end of the pool in a supine (on your back) streamlined position.

● They should then proceed by performing a full stroke backstroke over the given distance, with great technique.

● When they have finished this drill, it's important to ensure that they allow the swimmers swimming behind them enough room to allow them to complete this drill.

6.4: Stroke count with fists

Purpose: This is the fourth in a series of stroke count drills, which can help the swimmer to improve their stroke count by the introduction of swimming with clenched fists.

How to perform this drill: The swimmer should start this drill from a push & glide from the wall at the end of the pool in a supine (on their back) streamlined position.

● They then proceed by performing full stroke backstroke for one length/lap of the pool at a steady pace, with great technique.

● The swimmer should clench their fists and then go through the 'establishing' 'reducing' and 'holding' stroke count drills.

● Often once the swimmer has completed these drills, when they go back to normal stroke counting with open hands, they may find that they have developed a better 'feel for the water' and as a result may be able to reduce their stroke count still further.

● When they have finished these drills, it's important to ensure that they allow the swimmers swimming behind them enough room to allow them to complete these drills.

6.5: Min-max drill

4 x 50m	Rep 1			Rep 2			Rep 3			Rep 4		
	Stroke Count	Time	Total	Stroke Count	Time	Total	Stroke Count	Time	Total	Stroke Count	Time	Total
Swimmer 1	30	36	66	32	34	66	30	34	64	32	32	64
Swimmer 2	26	32	58	26	30	56	28	28	56	28	30	58
Swimmer 3	32	36	68	32	34	66	30	34	64	30	32	62
Swimmer 4	24	28	52	24	26	50	26	24	50	26	22	48

Purpose: This is the last in a series of stroke count drills.

- The objective of this drill is to swim a given distance with the minimum amount of arm strokes with the maximum amount of speed.

How to perform this drill: For example, over 4 x 50m: A swimmer completes the first repetition (rep) in a time of 30 seconds with a stroke count of 36.

- By adding the number of seconds, it took to complete the rep, to the number of strokes it took to complete the rep, this gives the swimmer a total 'stroke efficiency score' of 66.
- The swimmer's objective for the next repetition is to reduce their stroke efficiency score by either swimming faster, taking fewer strokes or a combination of both. (see table above)
- When they have finished this drill, it's important to ensure that they allow the swimmers swimming behind them enough room to allow them to complete this drill.

.

Chapter 7: Leg Kick

Introduction: Kicking is an important and sometimes undervalued key swimming skill, and as such should be constantly and consistently practised.

● An effective leg kick raises the swimmer's hips to just under the surface, thus reducing drag.

● As the leg muscles are amongst the largest in the body, having a trained, effective leg kick minimises energy and oxygen consumption, whilst maximising propulsion.

The key components for an effective leg kick

● Kicking should be initiated from the swimmer's thighs (quads), hamstrings and buttocks (glutes), using the largest muscles in the body to drive propulsion.

● There should be minimal knee bend, one of the most common faults while flutter (backstroke) kicking.

● Kicking with a bent knee increases drag and uses the relatively smaller calf muscles.

● The swimmer's feet should be in a pointed (plantar flexion) position.

● Lack of flexibility in the swimmer's ankles, can reduce effective propulsion.

7.1: Vertical kicking

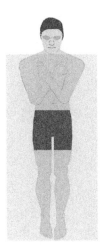

Purpose: Vertical flutter kicking is a great introductory kicking drill which can also help to improve the swimmer's ankle flexibility.

How to perform this drill: The swimmer should start this drill in a vertical position, in water deep enough so they cannot touch the bottom.

• They should perform a slow and steady backstroke leg (flutter) kick.

• They should fold their arms across their chest.

• They should ensure that they keep their chin level on the surface.

• The swimmers should initiate the kick from their thighs (quads), hamstrings and buttocks (glutes).

• They should focus on eliminating any knee bend.

• Younger and inexperienced swimmers may find it useful to use fins or a kickboard when first learning this drill.

Variations: The swimmer can increase the intensity of their leg kick, in three stages

• Level1: By raising their shoulders out of the water.

• Level 2: By raising their hands and forearms out of the water.

• Level 3: By raising their arms out of the water, above their head in a streamlined position.

7.2: Kicking with kickboards

Purpose: This drill introduces the swimmer to the backstroke leg kick action, in a supine position (on their back).

How to perform this drill: The swimmer should start this drill from a push & glide in a horizontal supine (on their back) position, while holding a kickboard in each hand and while performing a gentle flutter kick.

● They should hold the far edge of each kickboard, with their forearms resting on the kickboard.

● Their arms should be bent at the elbow at an approximately ninety-degree angle.

● The swimmers should initiate the kick from their thighs (quads), hamstrings and buttocks (glutes).

● They should focus on eliminating any knee bend.

● They should complete this drill for one length/lap of the pool (25m).

7.3: 'Teddy bear' kicking

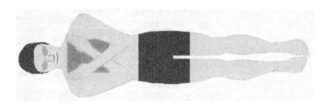

Purpose: This drill helps to further develop the swimmer's leg kick action.

How to perform this drill: The swimmer should start this drill from

a push & glide in a horizontal supine (on their back) position.
- They should hold a kickboard across their chest, as if they are cuddling a 'teddy bear' and while performing a gentle flutter (backstroke) kick.
- The swimmer should initiate the kick from their thighs (quads), hamstrings and buttocks (glutes).
- They should focus on eliminating any knee bend.
- They should complete this drill for one length/lap of the pool (25m).

7.4: Kicking 'hands in pockets'

Purpose: This drill helps to further develop the swimmer's leg kick action.

How to perform this drill: The swimmer should start this drill from a push & glide in a horizontal supine (on their back) position, while performing a slight flutter (backstroke) kick.
- The swimmer's arms should be by their sides ('hands in pockets').
- The swimmer should initiate the kick from their thighs (quads), hamstrings and buttocks (glutes).
- They should focus on eliminating any knee bend.
- They should complete this drill for one length/lap of the pool (25m).

Variation: Once mastered the swimmer can then help develop their leg kick still further, by placing their hands on their buttocks while performing this drill.

7.5: Streamlined kicking

Purpose: This drill helps to further develop the swimmer's leg kick action.

How to perform this drill: The swimmer should start this drill from a push & glide in a horizontal streamlined supine (on their back) position, while performing a slight flutter kick.
● The swimmer should initiate the kick from their thighs (quads), hamstrings and buttocks (glutes).
● They should focus on eliminating any knee bend.
● They should complete this drill for one length/lap of the pool (25m).
Coaching point: Whilst performing this drill the swimmer should engage their core*, to help ensure that their back, buttocks and hips are raised up to just below the surface.
Variations: Once mastered the swimmer can increase the resistance by, placing their hands on the top of their head, thus ensuring their forearms push against the water.

*How to engage your core
To engage their core, the swimmer should continue to breathe normally.
● They should then tighten/contract their stomach muscles while drawing their navel towards their spine.

7.6: Clapping hands

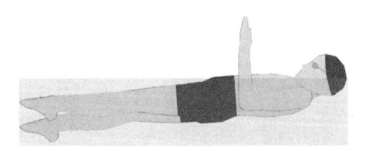

Purpose: This drill helps to further develop the swimmer's leg kick action, by adding increased resistance by clapping their hands while performing this drill.
How to perform this drill: The swimmer should start this drill from a push & glide in a horizontal supine (on their back) position, while performing a steady flutter kick.
● The swimmer should 'pin' their elbows to their sides and proceed to clap their hands.
● The swimmer should initiate the kick from their thighs (quads), hamstrings and buttocks (glutes).

- They should focus on eliminating any knee bend.
- They should complete this drill for one length/lap of the pool (25m).

Coaching Points: The swimmer should focus on their leg kick while they clap their hands.

7.7: Kickboard over the knees

Purpose: This drill helps to further develop the swimmer's leg kick action, by helping them to reduce any excessive knee bend, during the leg kick.

How to perform this drill: The swimmer should start this drill from a push & glide in a horizontal supine (on their back) position, while holding a kickboard in both hands over their knees.

- The swimmer should initiate the kick from their thighs (quads), hamstrings and buttocks (glutes).
- They should focus on eliminating any knee bend.
- The swimmer should focus on not bending their knees at the end of the kicking action as the foot comes up to just break the surface.
- Kicking with a bent knee increases drag and uses the relatively smaller calf muscles.
- They should complete this drill for one length/lap of the pool (25m).

7.8: Lateral kicking

Purpose: To further help develop the swimmer's leg kick, by introducing them to lateral kicking.

- This is an important part of the full stroke, by providing secondary propulsion during the rotation of the swimmer's body.

How to perform this drill: The swimmer should start this drill from

a push & glide in a horizontal supine (on their back) position, while performing a slight flutter kick.
● They should have their right arm fully outstretched and their left arm by their side.
● The swimmer should then slowly and smoothly rotate their body to an approximate thirty degrees angle, on their right-hand side.
● They should hold this position, while they perform six flutter kicks.
● They should then slowly and smoothly rotate their body to an approximate thirty degrees angle, on their left-hand side, with their left arm fully outstretched and perform a further six flutter kicks.
● The swimmer should continue this drill using alternating arms for one length/lap of the pool.

7.9: Kick builds

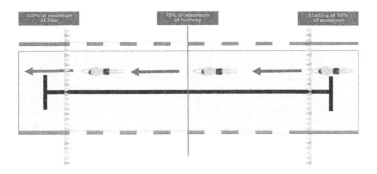

Purpose: This is an introductory drill to kicking speed play, which can help strengthen and develop the swimmer's backstroke leg kick.

How to perform this drill: The swimmer should start this drill from a push & glide in a horizontal streamlined supine (on their back) position, while they perform a steady leg kick.
● The swimmer should start kicking at approximately 50% of their maximum leg kick speed.
● They should gradually increase the speed of their kick over one length/lap.
● The swimmer should be at approximately 75% of their maximum leg kick speed at half-way.
● Without deterioration of their kicking technique, the swimmer should be close to reaching their maximum leg kick speed as they approach the finish of the length/lap.
● They should focus on kicking from their thighs (quads), hamstrings and buttocks (glutes).

- The swimmer should also focus on eliminating any knee bend.
- They should ensure that their feet are in a pointed (plantar flexion) position.
- Younger and inexperienced swimmers may find it useful to use fins when first learning this drill.

7.10: Kicking speed play

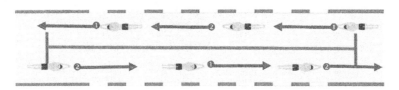

Purpose: This is a further speed play drill to help develop and strengthen the swimmer's leg kick.

How to perform this drill: The swimmer should start this drill from a push & glide in a horizontal streamlined supine (on their back) position.

- They should proceed to perform ten slow, drill paced (flutter) leg kicks (figure 1).
- They should then proceed to perform ten fast sprint paced leg kicks (10/10) (figure 2).
- This drill should be repeated initially over 50m.

Variations: Once mastered this drill can be made more difficult by progressively reducing the number of slow and fast leg kicks i.e. seven slow leg kicks, then seven fast leg kicks (7/7).

Chapter 8: Underwater Dolphin Kicking

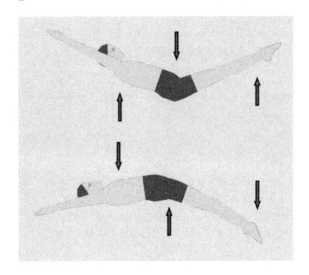

Introduction: Underwater dolphin kicking has become an increasingly important swimming skill, playing a key part during backstroke starts and turns, where the swimmer can swim underwater for 15m per length.
● Therefore, it's possible to swim further underwater than swimming backstroke full stroke when swimming short course (in a 25m pool).

The trained and effective underwater dolphin kick is usually quicker than performing full stroke backstroke on the surface.
● Many coaches refer to underwater dolphin kicking as the 'fifth stroke'.
● Many of the world's top swimmers regularly practice and develop their underwater dolphin kicking technique during training.
● Underwater dolphin kicking should be a key part of every competitive swimming programme.

Coach Arthur says: Water up your nose? "Some swimmers find that while performing these drills, water goes up their nose.
● To help prevent this, the swimmer can either use a nose clip.
● Some swimmers prefer breathing in then puffing out their cheeks.
● This dilates their nostrils which can prevent the water from entering their nose".

The key components for an effective underwater dolphin kick are:
● An underwater dolphin kick should be performed in a tight streamlined position, to reduce drag.
● The swimmer should engage their core.
● The legs should be together, and the feet should be in a pointed (plantar flexion) position.
● This reduces drag and places the feet in the optimum position for maximum propulsion.
● The swimmer should focus on their trickle breathing technique (see below).
● The swimmer should focus on undulating their body from their chest, through their hips and their legs.
● They should start the undulation cycle by raising their chest, which lowers the hips, which in turn naturally raises their legs.
● They should complete the undulation cycle by, pressing downwards with their chest, which raises their hips, which in turn lowers their legs.
● It may be beneficial for younger or less experienced swimmers to wear fins while they master these drills.
Coach Arthur says: "Please note that when performing underwater dolphin kicking, that the upward leg kick provides the main propulsive force".

How to engage your core

Purpose: Engaging your core muscles ensures they are correctly aligned, to help support and perform certain swimming drills and skills effectively.

● To engage their core, the swimmer should continue to breathe normally.

● They should then tighten/contract their stomach muscles while drawing their navel towards their spine.

Core strength development

Purpose: To effectively engage their core whilst performing underwater dolphin kicking, the swimmer should develop their core strength.

● The swimmer should perform core development training exercises such as crunches and planks as a regular part of their dryland/land training programme.

Trickle breathing

● Trickle breathing is a breathing technique that can enable the swimmer to stay longer underwater while performing underwater dolphin kicking during their starts and turns.

● It requires the swimmer to take a large quick breath, then to slowly exhale in the water via their nose or their mouth.

8.1: Trickle breathing development poolside

Introduction: This drill introduces the swimmer to trickle breathing, which aids the development of an effective underwater dolphin kick.

How to perform this drill: This drill should be practised on the poolside/deck in a safe place away from the pool's edge.

● The swimmer should start this drill by taking a large quick breath, which fills their lungs.

● They should then put up their hand.

- The swimmer should then breathe out very slowly, via their nose or mouth ('trickle breathe') until they have no breath left.
- When they are out of breath, they should quickly lower their hand.
- The coach should time and record this drill.
- This should demonstrate to the swimmer that by adopting trickle breathing, they have enough time to perform underwater dolphin kicking efficiently.

8.2: Trickle breathing development pool

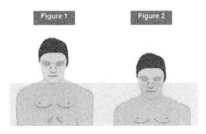

Purpose: This drill introduces the swimmer to trickle breathing in the water.

How to perform this drill: The swimmer should start this drill by standing up straight in the water.

- They should then bend their knees, lowering themselves into the water until their chin is touching the surface.
- They then take a large quick breath, which completely fills their lungs.
- Then the swimmer should lower themselves still further into the water until the line of the water has covered both their nose and mouth and is just below the rim of their goggles.
- They should start to breathe out very slowly, via their nose or mouth ('trickle breathe') until they have no breath left
- The swimmer should then raise themselves in the water and repeats this drill six times.

8.3: Vertical underwater dolphin kicking

Purpose: This is a great introductory drill for underwater dolphin kicking.

How to perform this drill: A diving pit or a pool with a deep end, is a great place for a swimmer to learn and practice vertical underwater dolphin kicking.

● The swimmer should start this drill by sinking to the bottom of the pool.

● They should then adopt a streamlined squat position.

● They should then drive up through their legs and perform fast and vigorous vertical underwater dolphin kicking, to shoot them through the water to the surface.

● The swimmer should ensure they are performing trickle breathing, to help them complete this drill.

● Once mastered the swimmer should try to increase the speed of their kicks.

● Younger and inexperienced swimmers may find it useful to use fins when first learning this drill.

8.4: Underwater dolphin kicking – introduction

Purpose: This is a further introductory drill to help develop and maintain an effective underwater dolphin kick.

How to perform this drill: The swimmer should start this drill from a push and glide from the end of the pool, in a horizontal streamlined supine (on their back) position, about half a metre under the surface.

● They should commence with this drill by initially performing six underwater dolphin kicks, to help them gauge the distance they can travel underwater.

● Once mastered they should gradually increase the number of kicks until they can perform this drill over 15m.

● The swimmer should ensure they increase their speed while discovering how many underwater dolphin kicks it takes them to reach 15m.

● This is the maximum distance a swimmer can travel legally underwater after a start or a turn.

● The swimmer should ensure they are performing trickle breathing, to help them complete this drill.

● Younger and inexperienced swimmers may find it useful to use fins when first learning this drill.

Variations: Further resistance can be added by the swimmer crossing their arms across their chest or folding their arms above their head while performing this drill.

8.5: Underwater 'corkscrew' dolphin kicking

Purpose: This drill can further help to develop and maintain an effective underwater dolphin kick, by the introduction of 'corkscrewing' through the water.

How to perform this drill: The swimmer should start this drill from

a push and glide from the end of the pool, in a horizontal streamlined supine (on their back) position, about half a metre under the surface.

● The swimmer should then perform an underwater 'corkscrew' dolphin kick.

● This is achieved by the swimmer kicking three underwater dolphin kicks on their back, three underwater dolphin kicks on their right-hand side, three underwater dolphin kicks on their front and three underwater dolphin kicks on their left-hand side.

● Once completed they should rise to the surface to take a breath, then return to approximately half a metre under the surface and repeat this drill.

● The swimmer should initiate their body rotation from their shoulders, trunk and hips.

● The swimmer should ensure they are performing trickle breathing, to help them complete this drill.

● They should complete this drill for one length/lap of the pool (25m).

Variations: Further resistance can be added by the swimmer crossing their arms across their chest or folding their arms above their head while performing this drill.

8.6: Sideways underwater dolphin kicking

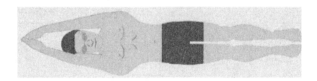

Purpose: This is an underwater dolphin kicking drill to help the swimmer to develop a powerful dolphin leg kick while on their side, which is required during a backstroke turn.

How to perform this drill:

● The swimmer should start this drill from a push and glide from the wall at the end of the pool, on their right-hand side.

● They should perform six underwater dolphin kicks on their right-hand side in a tight streamlined position, approximately half a metre under the surface.

● Once completed they should rise to the surface to take a breath, then return to approximately half a metre under the surface and repeat the drill.

● The swimmer should ensure they are performing trickle breathing, to help them complete this drill.

● They should complete this drill for one length/lap of the pool (25m).

● They should repeat this drill by underwater dolphin kicking on their left-hand side.

Variations: Resistance can be added by the swimmer crossing their arms across their chest or folding their arms above their head while performing these drills.

8.7: Underwater dolphin kicking - tempo drill

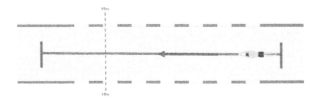

Purpose: This is an introductory underwater dolphin kicking speed development drill, which can help the swimmer establish the most effective tempo/speed for their kick.

● If a swimmer performs underwater dolphin kicks that are too big, then this may increase drag/resistance.

● However, if a swimmer performs underwater dolphin kicks that are too small, then this may not be an effective means of propulsion.

● The optimum underwater dolphin kick for most swimmers is somewhere in between.

How to perform this drill: The swimmer should start this drill from a push and glide from the end of the pool, in a horizontal streamlined supine (on their back) position, about half a metre under the surface.

● They should then perform fast and vigorous underwater dolphin kicking over a distance of 15m.

● The swimmer should count the number of underwater dolphin kicks they require to complete this distance.

● This is the maximum distance a swimmer can travel legally underwater after a start or a turn.

● The coach should record the time they take to complete this distance and feed this information back to the swimmer.

● The swimmer may need to adjust the depth of their kick and tempo until they achieve their optimum time.

● The swimmer should ensure they are performing trickle breathing, to help them complete this drill.

● Younger or less experienced swimmers may need to use fins when first learning this drill.

8.8: Underwater dolphin kicking - shooters drill

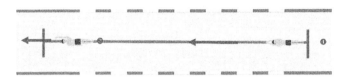

Purpose: This is an excellent drill for further developing and maintaining the swimmer's underwater dolphin kicking speed, while introducing them to the transition into a full stroke.

How to perform this drill: The swimmer should start this drill from a push and glide from the end of the pool, in a horizontal streamlined supine (on their back) position, about half a metre under the surface.

● The swimmer should then perform ten underwater dolphin kicks at maximum speed (figure 1).

● They should then breakout to the surface and sprint full stroke backstroke for the remainder of the length/lap (25m) (figure 2).

● The underwater dolphin kicks should be performed as quickly as possible and the breakout should be shallow enough to allow the smooth transition into a sprint backstroke stroke.

● The swimmer should ensure they are performing trickle breathing, to help them complete this drill.

● Once mastered the swimmer should perform underwater dolphin kicks to 15m.

● This is the maximum distance a swimmer can travel legally underwater after a start or a turn.

Chapter 9: Speed Development

Introduction: Since backstroke is performed on the back, swimmers cannot engage as many of their body's larger muscle groups as they can while performing either freestyle or butterfly.
● To compensate for this, backstroke should be performed at a high tempo with a fast stroke rate.

The introduction of varying speeds (speed play) into a training programme, helps to develop the swimmer's ability to swim at varying tempos.
● This is an important part of the development of a swimmer's training and eventually their race tactics.
● This type of training can be tough but is a useful method of increasing a swimmer's fitness.

The key components for effective speed development are:
● The swimmer should be able to swim at varying speeds, without the deterioration of technique.
● They should place the emphasis on varying their speed and not varying their effort.
● As for sprint training, speed play requires a lot of effort at maximum, or near to maximum speed. Therefore, swimmers may require more rest than usual.
● For tougher sets, swimmers may require one-part work to one-part rest: i.e. 30 seconds speed development and 30 seconds rest, or even more.

Breathing
● A regular breathing pattern can help increase the tempo of the

stroke.
- The swimmer should avoid holding their breath.
- Ideally, they should inhale as one arm passes their ear and exhale as the other arm passes their other ear.

9.1: Backstroke arms butterfly legs

Purpose: This drill helps develop the swimmer's stroke rate, by the introduction of a butterfly leg kick.

How to perform this drill: The swimmer should start this drill from a streamlined push and glide from the wall at the end of the pool, in a horizontal streamlined supine (on their back) position.

- The swimmer should proceed to perform a backstroke arm stroke with a dolphin leg kick.
- The swimmer should ensure they perform one arm pull to one leg kick.
- They should inhale as one arm passes their ear and exhale as the other arm passes their other ear.
- Although the butterfly leg kick can restrict the swimmer's shoulder, trunk and hip rotation, they should still focus on achieving a smooth body rotation.
- They should complete this drill for one length/lap of the pool (25m).

9.2: Spin drill

Purpose: This drill furthers help to further develop a faster stroke rate.

How to perform this drill: The swimmer should start this drill from a push and glide from the wall at the end of the pool.

● They should proceed by raising their knees and trunk into a semi-recumbent sitting position, with their body at approximately forty-five degrees.

● They should continue this drill by performing a steady and controlled backstroke arm pull in a 'tucked' (semi-recumbent) position for six strokes.

● Then they should perform the next six arm strokes as quickly as possible.

● The swimmer should then proceed to recover by performing six steady and controlled arm strokes, before returning to perform another six quick arm strokes.

● Some swimmers may find it easier to sit in a more upright position.

● They should repeat this drill for one length/lap of the pool (25m).

9.3: Swim builds

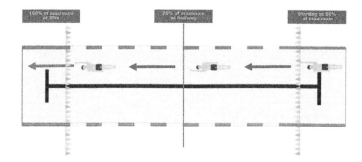

Purpose: This drill is an excellent introduction to swimming backstroke at a gradually increased speed.

How to perform this drill: The swimmer should start this drill from a streamlined push and glide from the wall at the end of the pool, in a horizontal streamlined supine (on their back) position.

● They should proceed by performing a steady full stroke backstroke.

● The swimmer should start swimming at approximately 50% of their maximum swimming speed.

● They should gradually increase the speed of their swim over one length/lap.

● The swimmer should be swimming at approximately 75% of their maximum swimming speed at half-way.

● Without deterioration of technique, the swimmer should be close to reaching their maximum swimming speed as they approach the finish of the length/lap.

● The swimmer should ensure that they gradually increase both their arms and leg speed to increase the overall speed of their swim.

● Increasing their leg speed should naturally increase their arm speed.

● Younger and inexperienced swimmers may find it useful to use fins when first learning this drill.

9.4: Backend/frontend swims

Purpose: These drills introduce the swimmer to race pacing and tactics.

- For backstroke races of 100m or over, the swimmer should develop an idea of how they are best going to swim their race.
- There are two basic methods of pacing a race.
- The first is to start at a steady pace and build speed towards the end of the race (backend swims).
- The second is to start quickly and try to maintain a fast pace for as long as possible (frontend swims).

How to perform a backend swims: This drill introduces the swimmer to swimming progressively faster over four lengths/laps of the pool (100m).

The swimmer should start this drill from a streamlined push and glide from the wall at the end of the pool, in a horizontal streamlined supine (on their back) position.

- They should proceed to swim full stroke backstroke at a steady pace.
- For the first length/lap (25m), this should be at approximately 70% of their maximum swimming speed.
- The second length/lap should be swum faster than the first length, at approximately 75% of their maximum swimming speed.
- The third length/lap should be quicker than the second length/lap, at approximately 80% of their maximum swimming speed.
- The last length/lap should be quickest of all, at their maximum swimming speed.
- Each of length/lap splits for this drill should be timed, recorded and if necessary adjusted.
- The coach should give feedback to the swimmer and future race

pace target timings adjusted accordingly.

● **Please note:** the objective of this drill is controlled speed, with great technique.

● The swimmer should focus on a fast and smooth stroke.

How to perform a frontend swims: This drill has the objective to help the swimmer to start fast and attempt to hold onto a fast pace, without too much drop off in time over four lengths/laps of the pool (100m).

● It can be far more difficult to judge the correct pacing of a frontend swim.

● The swimmer should start this drill from a streamlined push and glide from the wall at the end of the pool, in a horizontal streamlined supine (on their back) position.

● For the first length/lap (25m), this should be at approximately 70-80% of their maximum swimming speed.

● Each of the swimmer's length/lap splits for this drill should be timed, recorded and future race pace target timings adjusted accordingly.

● The coach should give feedback to the swimmer and future race pace target timings adjusted accordingly.

● **Please note:** the objective of this drill is controlled speed, with great technique.

● The swimmer should focus on a fast and smooth stroke.

9.5: Race pace development set

Purpose: This is a great race pace set for developing the swimmer's ability to perform even-paced, frontend and backend swims.

● An even-paced swim: These are performed at the same pace throughout.

● A frontend swim: These are performed faster at the beginning of the race than at the end.

● A backend swim: These are performed faster at the end of the race than at the beginning.

How to perform this set: The swimmer should start this drill from a streamlined push and glide from the wall at the end of the pool, in a horizontal streamlined supine (on their back) position.

● This set should be performed as 6 x 300m broken swims.

● As a 200m at race pace, with a 15-second rest interval

● This should be followed by a 100m recovery swim, with a one-minute rest interval.

Reps 1 & 2: Even paced swims

Reps 3 & 4: Frontend swims

Reps 5 & 6: Backend swims

● Each of the swimmer's race pace length/lap splits should be timed, recorded and future race pace target timings adjusted accordingly.

● The coach should give feedback to the swimmer and future race pace target timings adjusted accordingly.

● **Please note:** the objective of this drill is controlled speed, with great technique.

● The swimmer should focus on a fast and smooth stroke.

9.6: Easy/fast swims

Purpose: This drill helps to develop the swimmer's ability to swim at varying speeds.

How to perform this drill: The swimmer should start this drill from

a streamlined push and glide from the wall at the end of the pool, in a horizontal streamlined supine (on their back) position.

● They should proceed at a steady drill pace, with great technique for half a length/lap.

● On reaching halfway, they should sprint for the remaining half of the length/lap, without the deterioration of technique.

● This drill can be reversed so that the swimmer sprints for half a length/lap and swims at drill pace for the remaining half a length/lap.

● Poolside/deck markers at halfway would greatly assist the swimmer during this drill.

9.7: Easy/fast strokes

Purpose: This drill helps to develop the swimmer's ability to swim short bursts at varying speeds.

How to perform this drill: The swimmer should start this drill from a streamlined push and glide from the wall at the end of the pool, in a horizontal streamlined supine (on their back) position.

● They should proceed at a steady pace (200m race pace), with great technique for three strokes.

● The swimmer should then sprint for another three strokes, again without the deterioration of technique.

● This drill should be repeated for a length/lap of the pool (25m).

Variation: This drill can be adapted to increase the number of strokes i.e. five strokes easy/ five strokes fast.

● This drill can be a tough set for some swimmers, so any increase in distance should be carried out gradually and only once they have adapted to its demands.

● For tougher sets swimmers may require 2 parts work to 1-part rest: i.e. 1-minute speed play and 30 seconds rest.

9.8: Speed play 6 X 50m

Slow	Sprint
40m	10m
40m	10m
25m	25m
25m	25m
10m	40m
10m	40m

Purpose: This speed play drill should be conducted over a series of 50m reps.

How to perform this drill: The swimmer should start this drill from a streamlined push and glide from the wall at the end of the pool, in a horizontal streamlined supine (on their back) position.

● They should perform a set of 6 x 50m off a suggested rep time of one minute.

● The timings can be adjusted accordingly.

● The swimmer should swim at either drill pace (slow) or sprint pace (fast), at varying distances over 50m.

● The first two reps should be performed as 40m slow and 10m fast.

● Reps three and four should be performed as 25m slow and 25m fast.

● The final two reps five and six, should be performed as 10m slow and 40m fast.

● Poolside/deck markers at 10m from the end of each length/lap and at halfway would greatly assist the swimmer during this drill.

9.9: Speed play reducing times

1 x 25m on 30 seconds
2 x 25m on 25 seconds
1 x 25m on 30 seconds
2 x 25m on 20 seconds
1 x 25m on 30 seconds
2 x 25m on 15 seconds
1 x 25m on 30 seconds

Purpose: This is a great speed play drill of increasing intensity over

10 x 25m.

How to perform this drill: The swimmer should start this drill from a streamlined push and glide from the wall at the end of the pool, in a horizontal streamlined supine (on their back) position.

● This drill starts with an easy-paced one length/lap swim on 30 seconds.

● This should be followed by two single lengths/laps on the reduced time of 25 seconds.

● This should be followed by another easy-paced one length/lap swim on 30 seconds.

● This should be followed by a further two single lengths/laps of further reduced times swims of 20 seconds.

● This should be followed by another easy-paced one length/lap swim on 30 seconds.

● The last two lengths/laps of reduced times swims should be performed at maximum speed on 15 seconds.

● This should be followed by a final an easy-paced one length/lap swim on 30 seconds.

Chapter 10: Starts

Introduction: Learning how to perform an effective backstroke start can be a slow process. ● There are several technical elements to a backstroke start which some swimmers find difficult to master.
● Therefore, as with all competitive starts, they should be practised consistently and persistently.

Backstroke is the only competitive stroke, where the swimmer starts in the water.
● Like all competitive strokes, the start is the fastest part of a swimmer's race, which requires the swimmer to explode off the starting block with great technique and power.

The competitive backstroke starting positions:

There are three common competitive backstroke starting positions.
● These are the tucked, neutral and extended positions.

The tucked starting position: Where the swimmer, pulls

themselves up to the block, with bent elbows and with their chin tucked onto their chest.

The neutral position: Where the swimmer, pulls themselves up to the block, with bent elbows and with their head in an upright/neutral position.

The extended position: Where the swimmer, pulls themselves up to the block, with straight arms and with their head extended upwards and slightly backwards.

The key elements of a great backstroke start are:

● On the starting signal, the swimmer should explode off the starting block.

This should be achieved by:

• Driving off the pool wall by powerfully extending their toes, legs and hips.

• Throwing their head backwards.

• Pushing off with their arms by flinging them backwards into a tight streamlined position.

• Adopting an arched back to facilitate a clean entry into the water.

• As soon as the swimmer enters the water, they should maintain the speed of the start by commencing with fast and vigorous underwater dolphin kicking.

• The swimmers should gradually rise to the surface and should breakout into their full stroke before the permitted 15m from the start.

Backstroke starts in more detail

Slipping off the wall

Many swimmers slip off the wall during a backstroke start.

• To prevent slipping, the swimmer should pay attention to the way they pull their body up to the block, the position of their feet on the pool wall and the way that they drive off the pool wall.

The hand position

The swimmer has several options concerning the placement of their hands.

• Most senior or experienced swimmers grip the starting block by the horizontal bar or if available, some adopt a wider arm stance by gripping the front legs of the starting block.

• However, younger and less experienced swimmers may have

trouble reaching up for the starting block and may prefer to use the swimming pool gutter or pool edge instead.

The pull-up

To prevent slipping when in the set position, the swimmer should push their bottom out so that their legs form a 90 degrees angle at their knees.
- This set position can take most of the weight off the swimmer's feet and distributes it more evenly over their entire body.

The feet position
The swimmer has several options concerning the placement of their feet during a backstroke start.
- Some swimmers prefer to place their feet out of the water.
- Some swimmers prefer to place their feet in a parallel position, others prefer to have one foot slightly higher than the other (a track start).
- Using a track start usually results in the start being a little deeper on entry.
- Younger or more inexperienced swimmers can start to develop their backstroke starts by placing their feet on the vertical line of the cross on the pool wall.
- These are usually found at the end of the lanes at many competitive swimming pools.
- Whatever their preferred feet position, swimmers should ensure that they are no further than shoulder-width apart.
- The swimmer should practice their backstroke starts using different feet positions until they find a position they prefer.

Coach Arthur says: "Please note, swimmers are not permitted to place their feet in or on the gutter. They are also prohibited to place their toes bent over the gutter lip".

The head position

The swimmer also has several options concerning the placement of their head, when in the set position.

● Some swimmers prefer to have their chin extended upwards and slightly backwards.

● While other swimmers prefer to have a neutral upright head position.

● Some swimmers prefer to have their head tucked in tight against their legs.

● The swimmer should practice their backstroke starts using the different head positions until they find a position they prefer.

Backstroke wedge

Some pools have the luxury of a backstroke starting wedge, which significantly reduces the chances of a swimmer slipping off the pool wall.

● This is a (wedge-shaped) device, which is attached to the starting block, usually by adjustable straps, and lowered into the water at the level of the swimmer's feet.

● These may be too expensive for some swimming clubs to use as a part of their swimming programme.

● However, coaches wherever possible should make these facilities available to help their swimmers develop their backstroke starting techniques.

Coach Arthur says Safety First: "If you are coaching younger or inexperienced swimmers, they should perform backstroke starts in deeper water (ideally 6 feet/2 metres) to ensure they don't hit their head on the pool bottom".

10.1: Drive & glide

Purpose: This is a great introductory backstroke start drill, which can help to develop the arching of the swimmer's back and the tight streamlining required towards the end of the start.

How to perform this drill: The swimmer should start this drill by performing a standard backstroke start, from the starting block.

● As they start to drive off the wall, from their toes, legs, hips and arms.

● They should focus on arching their back and adopting a tight streamlined position.

● The swimmer's head, arms body and legs should enter the same piece of water to reduce drag.

● The swimmer should hold a tight streamlined position until the momentum of the drive off the pool wall has ended.

● Ideally, the coach should mark the distance on the poolside/deck.

● The swimmer then has the objective of going a greater distance during further attempts.

10.2: No arms start

Purpose: The purpose of this drill is to further develop the explosive drive required from the swimmer's toes, legs and hips.

How to perform this drill: The swimmer should start this drill by performing a standard backstroke start, from the starting block.

• As they start to drive off the wall, from their toes, legs and hips.

• They should tuck their arms by their sides, helping them focus on their lower body drive off the pool wall, without the assistance of their arms.

• Ideally, the coach should mark the distance on the poolside/deck.

• The swimmer then has the objective of going a greater distance during further attempts.

10.3: Over the lane rope

Purpose: The purpose of this drill is to further develop the explosive drive from the toes, legs, thighs and arms, as well as developing an arched back, all essential for a great backstroke start.

How to perform this drill: The swimmer should start this drill by standing in waist-deep water.

● They should then position themselves with their backs to a lane rope/line (secured at both ends of the pool).

● When it's safe to do so, the swimmer should bend their knees, so they are now chest-deep in the water.

● Then the swimmer should drive off the pool floor, using their toes, legs, hips and arms upwards

● While doing so, they should arch their back and go backwards over the lane rope/line.

Coach Arthur says, Safety First: "As for all of these drills, please ensure the swimmers have enough room to perform them correctly and safely".

10.4: Backstroke start with underwater dolphin kicking

Purpose: The purpose of this drill is to further develop the backstroke start, by the introduction of underwater dolphin kicking.

● This helps to maintain the speed created by the start and transfers that speed into the breakout and the transition into the full stroke.

How to perform this drill: The swimmer should start this drill by performing a standard backstroke start, from the starting block.

● As they start to drive off the wall, from their toes, legs, hips and arms.

● They should arch their back and adopt a tight streamlined position.

● The swimmer's head, arms body and legs should enter the same piece of water to reduce drag.

● The swimmer should hold a tight streamlined position and commence fast and vigorous underwater dolphin kicking.

● They should commence with this drill by initially performing six underwater dolphin kicks, to help them gauge the distance they can travel underwater.

● Once mastered they should gradually increase the number of

kicks until they can perform this drill over 15m.
- Ideally, the coach should mark the distance on the poolside/deck.
- The swimmer then has the objective of going a greater distance during further attempts.

Also see underwater dolphin kicking chapter 8

10.5: Timed backstroke starts

Purpose: This drill helps to further develop an effective competitive start, by the timing and recording of the swimmer's start.

How to perform this drill: A swimmer performs a backstroke start at race pace.
- The coach should stand at the poolside/deck at 15m where a marker should be placed.
- As the swimmer passes the marker with their head, the coach should stop their stopwatch and record the result.
- The coach should give the swimmer feedback, regarding the time achieved, any technical adjustments that may be needed and praise the good things about their start.

Coach Arthur says: "The swimmer should remember that underwater dolphin kicking is faster than the backstroke stroke.
- Therefore, it should be regularly practised, to take maximum advantage of the 15m underwater dolphin kicking they are allowed from the start".

Chapter 11: Turns

Introduction: The backstroke turn can be problematic to coach or teach, as for some, this can cause some trepidation, as the swimmer cannot see the wall into which they are turning.

• Therefore, the backstroke turn should be broken down into a series of drills to overcome any possible anxiety.

Coach Arthur Says, Safety First: "If you are coaching or teaching younger or inexperienced swimmers while performing backstroke turn drills, you may wish to hold a large foam mat/float or kickboard on the pool wall as an extra safety measure and confidence booster".

The key elements of a great backstroke turn

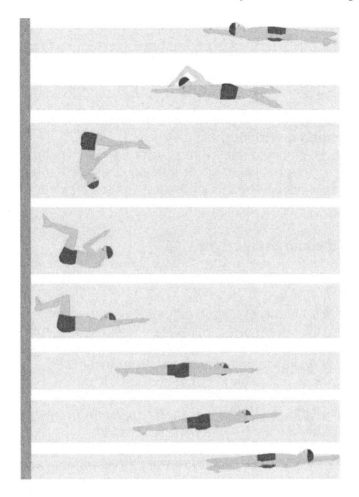

A fast approach
● The swimmer should not reduce their swimming speed when approaching the wall, thus reducing the efficiency of the turn.
● In fact, some of the world's top swimmers increase their speed into the pool wall.

A fast and smooth transfer from the backstroke position onto their front
● The swimmer should quickly and smoothly transfer themselves from the backstroke position over onto their front, to perform a backstroke turn.
● They should practice transferring from the backstroke position over onto their front, using either hand.

Establish a stroke count from the backstroke turn flags
● The swimmer should practice establishing the number of strokes they require from the backstroke turn flags to their turn at the pool wall.

A straight and fast flip/tumble turn
● The swimmer should perform a straight and fast flip/tumble turn.
● This should be achieved by performing a fast, full and powerful freestyle arm pull and by quickly tucking in their knees and chin to their chest.

Planting the feet firmly on the wall
● The swimmer should ensure that their feet are firmly planted on the pool wall, ideally, shoulder-width apart, which should help with an effective push-off.
● To facilitate an effective push-off the pool wall, swimmers should ensure that their knees are bent at approximately 90 degrees.
● If the swimmer is too close to the pool wall, it may require them to use extra energy to perform an effective push-off.
● If the swimmer is too far from the pool wall, it may result in a less powerful and effective push-off.
● There could also be a danger of the swimmer missing the pool wall altogether, resulting in their disqualification.

Push-off
● The swimmer should push-off the pool wall in a tight streamlined position, parallel to the pool's surface.

Transition
● As soon as the swimmer has pushed off the pool wall, they should maintain the speed of their turn by commencing fast and vigorous underwater dolphin kicking.

Breakout
● As soon as the swimmer starts to feel the momentum of the turn slowing down, they should start their arm action while the body is still submerged, to help bring their head to the pool's surface.

11.1: Backstroke to freestyle

Purpose: This drill introduces the swimmer to rotating from their back onto their front to enable them to perform a backstroke turn.

How to perform this drill: The swimmer should start this drill from a push and glide from the end of the pool, in a horizontal streamlined supine (on their back) position.

● They should commence with this drill by performing a full backstroke.

● Once the swimmer has completed three backstroke arm strokes, they should smoothly rotate their body onto their front (prone).

● The swimmer should now complete three freestyle arm strokes, after which they should completely rotate their body onto their back (supine).

● The swimmer should continue to repeat this drill for one length/lap of the pool.

11.2: Mid-pool backstroke turns

Purpose: This is a great drill for further developing the rotation on to the swimmer's front while performing a series of mid-pool backstroke turns.

How to perform this drill: The swimmer should start this drill from a push and glide from the end of the pool, in a horizontal streamlined supine (on their back) position.

● They should commence with this drill by performing five backstroke strokes.

● They should then completely rotate their body onto their front (prone).

● Then they should perform a fast, full and powerful freestyle stroke, which should help them, perform a mid-pool tumble/flip turn.

● After they have performed the mid-pool tumble/flip turn, they

should then rotate their body from the prone position back to a supine position, to repeat this drill.
• The swimmer should complete a series of mid-pool turns while completing one length/lap of the pool.
• They should start each rep of this drill using alternate hands.

11.3: Stroke count from the turn flags

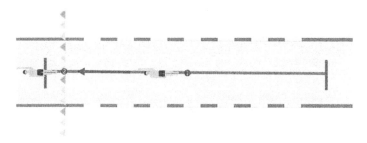

Purpose: This drill helps to develop the swimmer's backstroke turn by introducing them to focusing on their approach.
• This can be achieved by counting the number of strokes it takes from the backstroke turn flags to the pool wall.
• The turn flags are usually positioned five metres away from the pool wall.
How to perform this drill: From mid-pool, the swimmer should perform a medium pace backstroke (figure 1).
• As they swim under the backstroke turn flags, the swimmer should start to count the number of individual arm strokes it takes from the turn flags to reach the end of the pool (figure 2).
• It's important that the swimmer should practice this stroke count drill, starting on alternate hands.
• This will help to ensure they can effectively transfer from the backstroke position over onto their front, using either hand.
• This drill should be repeated until the swimmer is confident and knows how many strokes, they require from the backstroke turn flags to the pool wall.
• Once mastered, the swimmer should perform this drill at race pace.

11.4: Turn to feet

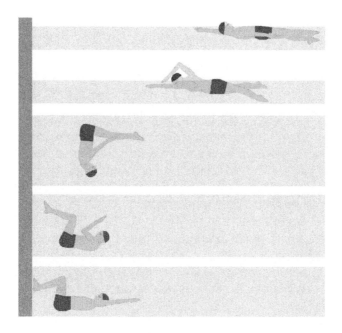

Purpose: To further help develop the swimmer's backstroke turn, by combining a stroke count and a 'turn to feet' drill.

How to perform this drill: The swimmer should start this drill from mid-pool by swimming backstroke into the pool end.

• As the swimmer swims under the turn flags, they should count two less individual arm strokes than they did when performing the 'stroke count from the turn flags' drill (see above).

• They should then perform a tumble turn.

• As soon as their feet touch the wall the drill is complete.

• The swimmer should focus on performing a fast turn.

• This should be achieved by performing a full and powerful freestyle arm pull and then quickly tucking in their knees, arms and chin to their chest.

• The higher the swimmer can place their feet on the wall the better, as this will facilitate a deeper push and glide, essential for an effective underwater dolphin kicking phase.

• If the swimmer is too far away from the pool wall, they may wish to try counting one less individual arm stroke, before turning.

11.5 Backstroke turn with underwater dolphin kick

Purpose: This drill helps to further develop the swimmer's backstroke turns, by the introduction of underwater dolphin kicking.
● This helps to maintain the speed created by the start and transfers that speed into the breakout and the transition into the full stroke.

How to perform this drill: The swimmer should start this drill by performing a standard backstroke turn.
● As the swimmer pushes off the wall, they should hold a tight streamlined position and commence fast and vigorous underwater dolphin kicking.
● They should commence with this drill by initially performing six underwater dolphin kicks, to help them gauge the distance they can travel underwater.
● Once mastered they should gradually increase the number of kicks until they can perform this drill over 15m.
● This is the maximum distance a swimmer can travel legally underwater after a start or a turn.
● Ideally, the coach should mark the distance on the poolside/deck.
● The swimmer then has the objective of going a greater distance during further attempts.

Also see underwater dolphin kicking chapter 8

11.6: Timed turns

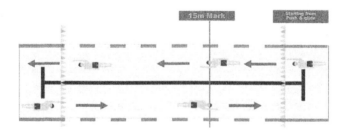

Purpose: This drill helps to further develop an effective turn, by the timing and recording of the swimmer's turn.

How to perform this drill: The swimmer should start this drill, from a push and glide in the supine position at the far end of the pool.

● The coach should stand at the poolside/deck, again 15m away from the turn end wall, where a marker or sinker should be placed on the poolside/deck.

● From a push and glide from the wall at the end of the pool, the swimmer should perform this drill, swimming at 100m race pace.

● As the swimmer's head passes the marker at 15m from their turn, the coach should start their stopwatch.

● Once the swimmer has performed their turn and has swum back past the 15m marker the coach should stop the stopwatch, record the result and feed the result back to the swimmer.

Coach Arthur says: "The swimmer should remember that underwater dolphin kicking is faster than the backstroke stroke.

● Therefore, it should be regularly practised, to take maximum advantage of the 15m underwater dolphin kicking they are allowed from the turn on each length/lap".

Chapter 12: Finishes

As with the backstroke turn, the backstroke finish can sometimes cause some trepidation for some swimmers, as they cannot see the wall into which they are finishing.
• Therefore, the backstroke finish should be broken down into a series of drills to overcome any possible anxiety.
• There can be significant time advantages to having an effective backstroke finish, and therefore backstroke finishing drills should be a regular part of any swimming programme.

The key elements of a great backstroke finish are:

A fast approach
• The approach to a backstroke finish, usually refers to the final 15m of a race.
• The swimmer should never look back at the pool wall, as this may significantly increase drag and reduce their swimming pace.
• The swimmer should maintain their race speed.
• In fact, some of the world's top swimmers increase their speed going into the pool wall.

The touch
• As the swimmer approaches the finish, they should lower their hand while keeping the arm fully extended.
• This should help the swimmer to slightly rotate their shoulders, trunk and hips, which facilitates a longer final stroke.
• Simultaneously the swimmer should lunge for the wall while

keeping the arm fully extended and while performing a powerful upward dolphin kick.

● The swimmer should ensure that while lunging for the pool wall, they do not shorten their final stroke by over-arching their back.

Coach Arthur Says: "To avoid disqualification, the swimmer should ensure that some part of their body is above the surface when they perform their touch".

Coach Arthur Says, Safety First: "If you are teaching or coaching younger or inexperienced swimmers while performing these backstroke finish drills, you may wish to hold a large foam mat, float or kickboard on the pool wall as an extra safety measure and confidence booster".

12.1: Mid-pool finish

Purpose: This drill introduces the swimmer to the combination of lunging for the finish with an upward dolphin kick.

How to perform this drill: The swimmer should start this drill from a push and glide from the wall at the end of the pool.

● The swimmer should then perform five full backstroke strokes, then they should perform a mid-pool lunge with a fully extended arm and a powerful upward dolphin kick.

● The swimmer should lower their hand while keeping the arm fully extended.

● They should slightly rotate their body onto the side of their extended arm.

● This should facilitate a longer final stroke.

● The swimmer should ensure that while lunging they do not shorten their extended arm by over-arching their back.

● The swimmer should repeat this drill for every five strokes.

● This will ensure that the swimmer can practice finishing with either hand.

12.2: Stroke count from the turn flags

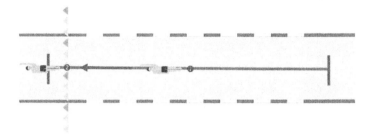

Purpose: This drill introduces the swimmer to a backstroke finish, by focusing on their approach and by counting the strokes it takes them from the backstroke turn flags to the pool wall.

How to perform this drill: From mid-pool, the swimmer should perform a medium pace full stroke backstroke into the pool wall.

• As they swim under the turn flags, the swimmer should count the number of individual arm strokes it takes them to reach the end of the pool.

• The swimmer should practice starting this drill on alternate hands, so they can effectively finish using either hand.

• The swimmer should repeat this drill until they are confident and know how many strokes they require.

Coach Arthur Says, Swimmers grow: "Please remember that swimmers grow and develop. They get stronger, faster and bigger, so their stroke count at the start of the season may be different to that at the season's end.

• Therefore, this drill should be practised regularly during the season".

12.3: Practice finish

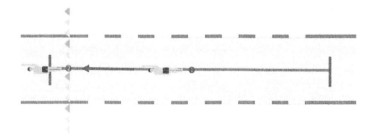

Purpose: This drill helps to further develop the swimmer's finish, by introducing them to finishing on the pool wall.

Please note: The swimmer should subtract one or two strokes from the original stroke count to allow for their lunge and upward dolphin kick into the wall.

How to perform this drill: The swimmer should start this drill from mid-pool.

• The swimmer should commence with this drill by performing a medium pace full stroke backstroke.

• As they swim under the turn flags, the swimmer should count the number of individual arm strokes it usually takes them to reach the end of the pool **BUT SUBTRACTS TWO STROKES.**

• The swimmer should then perform a lunge with a fully extended arm and a powerful upward dolphin kick.

• They should ensure that some part of their body is above the pool's surface when they perform their touch, to avoid possible disqualification.

• Once the swimmer has performed their finish the coach should feedback the results to the swimmer, along with any technical adjustments they think may help.

• It may be that the swimmer was too far away from the pool wall, in which case the swimmer should repeat the drill but only subtracting one stroke.

12.4: Timed finish

Purpose: This drill helps to further develop an effective racing finish by the timing and the recording of the swimmer's finish.

How to perform this drill: The swimmer should start this drill, from a push and glide from the wall at the far end of the pool, at 100m race pace.

• The coach should stand at the poolside/deck, 15m away from the turn end wall, where a marker should be placed on the poolside/deck.

BACKSTROKE Competitive Swimming Drills

- As the swimmer's head passes the marker 15m from their turn, the coach will start their stopwatch.
- Once the swimmer has performed their finish the coach should

Chapter 13: Warm-Up & Cool-down

Introduction: The importance of effective warm-ups and cool-downs is well documented, although it is still an area often overlooked in many training programmes.

● Before training and competition, the swimmer's muscles should be warmed, and their heart should be prepared to enable it to pump oxygen-rich blood throughout their body.

● After training and competition, the swimmer should perform an effective cool-down to aid muscle repair and help their recovery between training sessions or competition.

● It's, therefore, important to the swimmer's performance, to develop individual warm-up and cool-down protocols, which can be tailored to the individual swimmer and adapted to most training or competitive situations.

Examples of training and competition warm-up and cool-down protocols:

Warm-up 1: Dryland warm-up (blood flow stretching):
● Usually conducted on the poolside/deck before entering the water.

● This is to help ensure that the swimmer's muscles have an adequate blood supply and are warm and supple before swimming.
Warm-up 2: The short pool warm-up:
● Sometimes swimmers only get a few minutes to warm-up in the pool.

● Therefore, it's important that the swimmer has developed an effective pre-planned short pool warm-up protocol.

- **Warm-up 3: The Championship pool warm-up:**
- When competing at a major event the swimmer usually gets up to an hour in the water to warm-up.

Warm-up 4: Pre-Race warm-up (blood flow stretching)
- A swimmer could have to wait for an hour or before their event.
- Therefore, it's important that the swimmers wake up their muscles and help increase the blood flowing through their body again.
- Ideally, this should be a 10-minute routine before the call up to their race.

Cool-down 1: Post competition swim down:
- After any intense swimming activity, the swimmer's body and their nervous systems should have time to repair and recover.
- Usually, the sooner the swimmer conducts their swim down the more effective the cool-down.

Cool-down 2: Post competition cool-down (blood flow stretching).
- Swim down facilities are not always available at every meet/gala.
- The swimmer should get into the habit of stretching, walking or skipping after their race, to help their body and nervous system repair and recover.

Key components for a warm-up, cool-down and recovery swims are:
- Slow, smooth and controlled swimming, with great technique.
- They should include stroke counting, drills and speed play.
- The swimmer should keep moving during their warm-up to ensure their muscles are properly warmed up and their blood starts to flow.

13.1: American warm-up drill - strokes

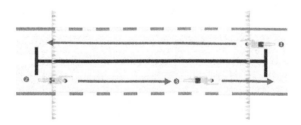

Purpose: This is an excellent warm-up drill, which requires the swimmer to perform a required number of strokes at a varying pace.
How to perform this drill: The swimmer should start this drill from a streamlined push and glide from the wall at the end of the pool, in a horizontal streamlined supine (on their back) position.

- The swimmer proceeds with this drill by performing eighteen strokes (each time the swimmer's hand enters the water) at drill pace, with their best technique (figure 1).
- They should then perform twelve strokes building to a 200m race pace (figure 2).
- Finally, they should perform six strokes holding a 200m race pace (figure3).
- This drill should be repeated for the distance of 200m.

13.2: American warm-up drill – distance

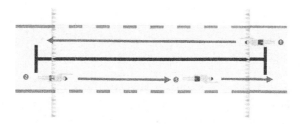

Purpose: This is an excellent warm-up drill, which requires the swimmer to swim certain distances at a varying pace.

How to perform this drill: The swimmer should start this drill from a streamlined push and glide from the wall at the end of the pool, in a horizontal streamlined supine (on their back) position.

- The swimmer proceeds with this drill by performing 75m at a drill pace, with their best technique (figure 1).
- They should then perform 50m building to a 200m race pace (figure 2).
- Finally, they should perform 25m holding a 200m race pace (figure 3).
- This drill should be repeated for the distance of 200m.

13.3: Super slow swimming

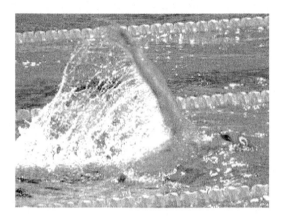

Purpose: Super slow swimming is an excellent cool-down drill to relax the swimmer and help them refocus on their technique.

How to perform this drill: The swimmer should start this drill from a streamlined push and glide from the wall at the end of the pool, in a horizontal streamlined supine (on their back) position.

● The swimmer should proceed with this drill by swimming as slowly as they can, with their best technique.

● This drill should be completed for one length/lap of the pool (25m).

Variation: The swimmer can add stroke counting to their super slow swimming, to add extra focus to the length of their stroke.

Chapter 14: Swimming Glossary

Introduction: Our swimming glossary contains a list of common competitive swimming terms with definitions, together with abbreviations and cross-references.

A

Aquatics: The collective (generic) name for any water-based competitive activity such as swimming, para-swimming, synchronised swimming, open water and water polo.

Aerobic Energy: The body's energy-producing system that requires oxygen.

Aerobic Training: The training system that requires oxygen. Usually involving long-distance swimming at a low intensity and a short rest interval.

Age Group Swimmers: Usually refers to swimmers under 16 years of age.

Anaerobic Energy: The body's energy-producing system that doesn't require oxygen.

Anaerobic Training: The training system that doesn't require oxygen. Usually involving short distance swimming at a high intensity and a long rest interval.

Anchor Leg: The final swimmer in a relay team.

Anchor Point: The point at the beginning of a stroke where the swimmer's hand starts to pull or push against the water at the beginning of the propulsive phase of the stroke.

Annual Training Plan: Usually formulated by the Head Coach during the closed season, this is an overall plan detailing the major objectives, championships and galas/meets for the up and coming season. It also outlines the different training periods for the season, together with an outline of what types of training activities should be performed.

Arm Stroke: The completion of an individual arm cycle, consisting of the pull phase, the exit phase and the recovery phase, before returning to the catch position at the start of the stroke.

Artistic Swimming see *Synchronised Swimming*

Ascending: Training set or rep on increasing times. Requiring a slower swim.

Assisted Training: Aided training that helps the swimmer go faster than normal training or race speed i.e. swimming with fins or being pulled by a rope.

Assisted Training: Any type of training that helps the swimmer to go faster i.e. swimming with fins or being pulled by a rope or bungee cord.

B

B/C: An abbreviation for backstroke.

B/S: An abbreviation for breaststroke.

Back End Scull: A scull which focuses on the last part of the stroke before it enters the recovery phase.

Backstroke Turn Flags: Flags that are suspended across the width of the pool, 5m from the pool end to indicate to swimmers during backstroke, that the pool end is approaching assist backstroke swimmers to gauge their turn.

Back-Up Time: The manual time which is given to a swimmer if they fail to stop the electronic timing system by not touching the timing pad hard enough or the pad fails to record a time.

BC: An abbreviation for Backstroke.

Beats Per Minute (BPM): The number of times that a swimmer's heartbeat per over one minute.

Best Stroke: see Main Stroke

Bilateral Breathing: A breathing pattern requiring the swimmer to breathe on both sides of their body, while swimming freestyle.

Blocks see Starting Blocks

Boxes: The place at galas/meets where entry cards must be handed in before the start of the warm-up.

BPM: An abbreviation for Beats Per Minute (Heart Rate)

BR: An abbreviation for breaststroke

Breakout: The transition from exiting underwater to the surface, from either a dive or turn into the full stroke.

Breath Control: Sometimes called 'hypoxia training' which limits the number of breaths a swimmer can take.

Broken Swims: Training sets usually in two parts, an intense phase and a recovery phase. i.e. 4 x 150m as: 100m target times PB + 15 Seconds on 2.00, 50m O/C recovery on 1.00

BS: AN abbreviation for Breaststroke.

Builds: A training set, which requires the swimmer to start at a slow pace, and then gradually 'builds' speed into the swim.

C

Call Room see Whipping Area

Carbohydrates: The main source of energy found in foods such as pasta and potatoes, that should be a large part of a swimmer's diet.

Catch: The part of an arm stroke where the swimmer's hand enters the water and 'anchors' their hand in position before they start to pull/scull at the front end of the stroke.

Chlorine: The chemical used in most swimming pools to kill germs and bacteria and help keep the water clean, clear and safe in which to swim.

Cooldown: A series of pool and poolside activities used by the swimmer after training or competition, essential for a swimmer's recovery and important for avoiding.

Cooldown Pool: A separate pool for swimming down after a competition, which is usually a teaching pool or diving pit.

Closing Date: The date when entries for a competition have to be received either by its organiser or the club's gala/meet secretary.

Club Championship: Premier internal club competition usually open to all members.

Conversion Times: Swimming times usually converted from short course to long course.

Core strength: A swimmer's core is the muscles in their abdomen, hips and lower back. These are developed to provide the swimmer better streamlining, power, endurance and range of movement.

Cross Training: Any type of training outside of the water, that compliments a swimmer's training programme.

D

Deck: see Poolside

Dehydration: The depletion of body fluids, usually caused by swimmers not drinking enough during training or competition. This is the most common cause of swimmers getting cramp and headaches.

Descending: Training set or rep on reducing times. Requiring a faster swim.

Development Gala/Meet: A gala/meet, to develop a swimmer's competition experience.

Did Not Compete (DNC): The initials used to indicate a swimmer who failed to compete in an event.

Did Not Finnish (DNF): The initials used to indicate a swimmer who failed to finish their event.

Did Not Start (DNS): The initial used to indicate a swimmer who did not start an event.

Disqualification Codes: These are codes used by gala/meet officials to indicate why and when an infringement of the rules has taken place, resulting in the swimmer's subsequent disqualification.

Disqualified (DQ): A swimmer is disqualified because, in the opinion of a poolside/deck official, they have infringed on the rules.

Distance per stroke: The amount of distance a swimmer covers during one complete stroke.

Diving Pit: A separate pool or a pool set off to the side of the competition pool. This pool has deeper water than a standard swimming pool, with diving boards/platforms. During a meet, this area may be designated as a swim-down pool.

DNC: see Did Not Compete

DNF: see Did Not Finish

DNS: see Did Not Start

Dolphin Kick: A kicking action used in butterfly, where the swimmer kicks with straight legs placed together.

Dorsiflexion: The foot position where it is flexed toward the front of the leg.

Double Arm Pull: A drill where the swimmer performs a pulling action with both arms pulling simultaneously.

Down sweep: see Sweep

DPS: An abbreviation for distance per stroke

DQ: see Disqualified

Drafting: Swimming behind another swimmer, to save energy. This technique is used frequently in open water swimming.

Drag: The resistance caused by the swimmer's head, body or limbs, as they move through the water

Drill Pace: A slow, smooth and steady swimming pace, to enable the swimmer to recover and/or learn/concentrate on their technique.

Drill: A series of exercises, drills and activities, used to develop a swimmer's stroke which focuses on a particular stroke and/or particular aspects of the stroke.

Dropped Time: When a swimmer goes faster than the previous performance they have 'dropped their time' or performed a personal best time.

Dryland Training: See Land Training

Dual Clubbing: Where a swimmer, usually due to educational commitments, swims for two clubs. One at or near their educational establishment and the second club is usually their original 'hometown' swimming club.

Dynamic Stretching: The type of stretching which requires the swimmer to stretch while performing full 'swinging' motions.

E

Easy & Smooth: Performing a swimming activity using minimum effort and with a great technique.

Easy: Performing a swimming activity using minimum effort.

EBP: Event Best Performance see Event Best Time.

EBT see Event Best Time.

Electronic Timing: A timing system which is operated electronically and linked to the touchpads in the water at the end of each lane. Most systems are linked to a scoreboard that displays the swimmer's times.

Entry Cards A swimmer receives an entry card from a competition organiser for each event that they have successfully applied. On arrival at the competition venue, the swimmer is required to 'post' these cards in a box to confirm their acceptance of their participation In relevant events.

Entry Deadline: A date when entries must be handed into either the host club or the club's competition secretary.

Entry Fees: The amount a swimmer is charged to enter an event. This fee varies from meet to meet.

Entry Limit: Each gala/meet may have a limit on the number of swimmers they can accept.

Entry Time: The event entry time a swimmer provides when applying to enter a competition.

Even Split: When a swimmer swims at an even pace during training or competition.

Evens: Reps within a set with even numbers.

Event Best Time: The best time recorded at a particular event, normally at an annual championship or gala.

Exit Phase: The phase of the arm stroke, after the pull phase and before the recovery phase, where the swimmer's hand leaves the water.

F
F/S: An abbreviation for freestyle.
False Start: Occurs when a swimmer leaves the starting block or is moving on the block before the starter starts the race. The swimmer will be disqualified for making a false start.
False Start Rope: see Recall Rope
Fartlek: 'Speed Play' a series of training swims at a varying pace, slow, medium and fast etc.
Fat: A source of food energy that should be a small part of a swimmer's diet.
Faulty Start: Occurs when a swimmer/s leaves the starting block due to an error of an official or failure of the starting equipment. Swimmer/s should not be disqualified in these instances.
File: A group of swimmers, swimming in a line, either in the same lane or on the same side of the lane.
Flexion: Bending of a limb or joint.
Flip turn: see Tumble Turn
Flutter Kick: A kicking action used in both Freestyle and Backstroke, where the swimmer kicks alternately with a straight leg kick.
Fly: An abbreviation for butterfly.
Foot Flexion: There are two types of foot flexion: pointing your foot (plantar flexion) and flexing it upwards (dorsiflexion).
Form Stroke: A collective term for either backstroke, breaststroke or butterfly.
Front Crawl: Another name used for freestyle.
Front End: A scull or drill performed at or to simulate the first part of the stroke.
FS: An abbreviation for freestyle.

G
Gala: A swimming competition
Goals: Short, medium and long-range aims & objectives set by swimmers at the start of each season and agreed by the coaches.
Grab Start: A start where the swimmer places their feet in a parallel position on the blocks.

H
Hand Timing: Timing system operated manually, by the use of

stopwatches.

HDW see Heat Declared Winner

Heart Rate Training: Training set where the swimmer is controlled by heart rate levels.

Heat Declared Winner (HDW) Commonly used in galas/open meets with a large entry list and schedule, where heats are arranged with swimmers seeded by their entry times. Once all the heats have been completed, the placings for each age group are calculated from the times recorded.

Heats: A race held at a competition, usually consisting of swimmers with similar submitted entry times.

High-Velocity Overload: Training swimming part of the length/lap (no more than 15m) at full speed without breathing, rest of the set distance swim easy

HR: An abbreviation of heart rate

HRT: An abbreviation of heart rate

HVO: An abbreviation of High-Velocity Overload

Hypertrophy: The increase in the size of organs (i.e. the heart) due to training.

Hypoxia Training see Breath Control

I

I.M. Order: The stroke order of an individual medley – butterfly, backstroke, breaststroke and freestyle.

I.M.: An abbreviation for Individual Medley.

In sweep: see Sweep

L

Ladder Swims: see Pyramid Swims

Land Training: Training conducted out of the water to gain additional benefits beyond those which can be achieved by training in the water alone. These include increased power, strength, endurance, speed, and coordination.

Lane Line: see Lane Rope

Lane Rope: The rope with floating markers that separate the individual swimming lanes.

Lap: see length.

Late Entries: Meet entries from a club or individual that are received by the meet host after the entry deadline. These entries are usually not accepted and are returned to the sender.

Lateral Position: Body and/or head position on the side.

Length: A single length/lap of a pool is 'there and back' usually 25m or 50m

Lesson Plan: The plan formulated by the coach as a guide to objectives of a swimming session. It details the sets and drills to be performed during a training session.

Logbook/Swimming Log: A journal/diary/log for keeping all the swimmers important swimming documentation in one place. Used for storing documentation such as goal setting sheets, recording training and competition performance evaluation sheets. This is an important monitoring system to aid a swimmer's development and should be kept by the swimmer and reviewed periodically by the Coach.

Long Bungee: Two bungees joined lengthwise, one end attached to the web belt, the other to a secure fixing.

Long Course: Competitions held in a 50m pool

M

Macrocycle: A training period of some 15 to 24 weeks, usually with a goal at the end of each cycle.

Main Set: The primary training set within a training session, focusing on the session's objectives.

Main Stroke: The swimmer's best stroke, sometimes referred to as their 'number 1' stroke.

Manual Time: The time for a swim recorded manually by a timekeeper using a stopwatch.

Marshalling Area: see Whipping Area

Masters Swimmers: Swimmers usually over 19 years old, who have their own dedicated training sessions and compete in their own dedicated competitions.

Maximum Distance per Stroke: A drill/drill, to develop a long, smooth stroke to develop stroke length.

MDPS: An abbreviation for Maximum Distance Per Stroke

Meet: see Gala

Mesocycle: A training period of some 1 to 6 weeks normally with its own training emphasis and objectives.

Microcycle: A short training period with its own training emphasis and objectives.

Midpoint: A scull or drill performed at or to simulate the middle part of the stroke.

Mins: An abbreviation for minutes.

Monitoring: Performed by coaches when either observing, recording or evaluating a swimmer's performance or technique in training and/or competition.

Monthly Training Plan: An outlined plan of the month's training activities and objectives.

N

National Qualifying Time: The qualifying time needed for entry to a national championship.

National Swimming Championships: The premium national swimming championships.

Negative Split: Swimming faster for the second half of the set distance than the first half

No Time Recorded (NRT): The abbreviation recorded on a heat sheet to indicate that a swimmer's time was not officially recorded.

NQT see National Qualifying Time

NTR see No Time Recorded.

Number 1 Stroke see Main Stroke

O

O/C: An abbreviation for own choice

Odds: Reps within a Set with even numbers.

Official Time: The swimmer's race time, usually recorded to one-hundredth of a second.

One Start Rule: Most competitions use the one start rule, which means that any swimmer responsible for a false start will be disqualified and not given a second chance to start.

Open Meet: Events that are 'open' to any qualified club or individual, although there may be a qualification standard/time.

Open Turn: A two-handed touch turn completed for Breaststroke and Butterfly

Open Water Swimming: Swimming that takes place outdoors either in the sea, rivers, lakes or docks etc.

OT see Official Time

Outsweep: see Sweep

Over the Top Start: To save time at some galas/meets for freestyle, breaststroke and butterfly races, the swimmers from the previous heat, may remain in the water until the next race starts.

Own Choice: A stroke or drill of the swimmer's choosing.

P

Pace Clock: A large free-standing or wall-mounted clock with a single hand used during training to give the swimmers a start time for a drill, sets and rest periods.

Para-Swimming: The specialist arm of swimming that caters for all those swimmers who have a disability and wish to train and compete.

PB: An abbreviation for Personal Best

Perceived Rate of Exertion (PRE): A subjective scale of effort assigned by the swimmer and/or coach, after training or competition.

Personal Best - The best time a swimmer has done so far in a particular stroke or event, either in training or competition.

Physiology: The scientific study of the functions in living systems and their parts.

Plantar Flexion: The foot position where the feet are in a pointed position, which reduces drag and places them in the optimum position for maximum propulsion.

Pool Floor Markings: The lines on the pool floor indicate the centre of a lane. The 'T' at the end of the black line indicates two metres from the end of the pool.

Poolside/: The area around the swimming pool reserved for swimmers, officials, and coaches.

Progression: A series of drills which when combined, breaks down into a 'progressive' order to help complete a more complex task.

Prone Position: A horizontal face-down body position.

Propulsion: The force that moves swimmers through the water.

Protein: Found in lean meat, milk and cheese, they are one of the main building blocks of body tissue and can also serve as a prime fuel source.

Pull Phase: The propulsive phase of the stroke performed underwater.

Pulse Rate: A method to monitor heart rate.

Push & Glide: Performed in the water at the start of a drill or drill. The swimmer 'pushes' off the pool wall with their feet, and glides in a streamlined position, to commence the exercise.

Pyramid: A training set where the workload/distance goes up then down.

Q
QT see Qualifying Time
Qualifying Time (QT): Times are necessary to enter most open meets, and all county, regional/state and national competitions. Some competitions will have upper and lower limits on their entry qualifying times.

R

Race Pace: Training at the same pace as the swimmer would race.

Rate of Perceived Exertion: a simple but effective method of monitoring and evaluating the intensity of a swimmer's performance during training and competition.

Recall Rope: A rope suspended across the width of the racing pool that is lowered to the water surface to stop swimmers, in the event of a false start.

Recovery Phase (arm/s): The part of the arm stroke, executed out of the water after the pull and exit phases, where both the arm and hand are returning to the catch position.

Recovery Phase (legs): The part of the leg kick is breaststroke that brings the swimmer's heels up to their buttocks.

Recovery: A drill, rep or set where the swimmer undertakes a slow and easy activity to allow the swimmer to recover from training.

Regional/State Qualifying Time (RQT): The qualifying time needed for entry to the regional/state swimming championship.

Relays: A swimming event in which four swimmers participate as a relay team. Each swimmer swimming an equal distance of the race. There are two types of relays: A Medley relay, where the first swimmer swims backstroke, the second swimmer swims breaststroke, the third swimmer swims butterfly and the last swimmer swims freestyle. The other type of relay is a freestyle relay, where all the swimmers swim freestyle.

Repetitions: A group of swims within a set.

Reps: An abbreviation for repetitions.

Resistance Training: A form of training with added resistance, to build either strength and/or stamina. i.e. using bungee/stretch cords.

Rest Interval: The period of rest and recovery during training between a set or a rep

RI: An abbreviation for a Rest Interval.

Rotation: A movement of the body in a forward (tucked) position when performing a tumble turn, or sideways when performing full stroke freestyle of backstroke.

RPE: An abbreviation for Rate of Perceived Exertion

RQT see Regional Qualifying Time

S
S/C see Stroke Count

S/L see Stroke Length

S/R see Stroke Rate

Scratch: To withdraw from an event after having declared an intention to participate.

Sculling: A swimming technique, focusing on the pitch and position of the swimmer's hands and forearms in the water, to achieve propulsion.

Secs: An abbreviation for seconds.

Set: see Training Set

Short Bungee: One bungee with one end attached to the web belt, the other to a secure fixing.

Short Course: Competitions held in a 25m pool

Sighting: An open water swimming navigation technique. Involving swimming with the head raised out of the water.

Signing In: Required at certain galas/meets where swimmers are required to 'sign in' against each event in which they are due to compete.

Signing Out: Required at certain galas/meets where swimmers are required to 'sign out' against each event they wish to withdraw from.

Sinker: A teaching device designed to sink to the bottom of the pool.

Skins: A swimming competition swam as an elimination event over several rounds.

Spearhead (Final): The lane order for spearheaded finals is decided from times in the heats or semi-finals. The fastest qualifier usually swims in lane 4, second fastest in lane 5, third in lane 3, fourth in lane 6, fifth in lane 2, sixth in lane 7, seventh in lane 1 and eighth in lane 8.

Speed Endurance: To perform at near maximum speed for a sustained period.

Speed Play: see Fartlek

Speeding Ticket: Awarded to a swimmer who swims too fast in a time graded gala/meet and will not be awarded points or medals.

Split: A portion of an event shorter than the total distance that is timed. i.e. a swimmer's first 25m or 50m time is taken as the swimmer swims their 100m race. It is common to take multiple splits for the longer distances and are used to determine if the swimmer is swimming at the correct race pace.

Sports Medicine: The branch of medicine dedicated to sports healing, prevention and rehabilitation.

Sports Psychology: The scientific study of the human mind and its functions in sport

Sports Science: The branch of science dedicated to sports performance.

Sprint Training: Training sets performed at faster than race pace.

Sprint: A swim at maximum pace.

SQT: State Qualifying Time see Regional/State Qualifying Time

Squad: A group of swimmers of roughly the same age and ability who train together.

Squadron: A freestyle relay of usually 10 or more swimmers in each team, arranged boy/girl in each age group, with the oldest swimmer going last.

Starting Block: The raised platform at the end of each lane of a competition pool, use for all competitive starts.

Starts: The start of a training set, gala/meet, either directly from the poolside/deck or in the case of backstroke an in the water start, usually with the aid of a starting block.

Static Stretching: The type of stretching which requires the swimmer to stretch while standing still. i.e. when touching their toes.

Step Test: A form of training 'test set' which helps monitor the swimmer's fitness.

Streamlined: The 'torpedo' position adopted by swimmers during a start and exiting a turn to reduce drag and achieve maximum speed and distance through the water.

Stretching see Dynamic Stretching and also Static Stretching

Stroke Count (S/C): Counting the number of strokes per length, to enhance stroke length and consistent swimming.

Stroke Length (S/L): The length in which a swimmer performs a single arm stroke.

Stroke Rate (S/R): The rate in which a swimmer performs several arm strokes within a given time.

Submitted Time: Times used to enter swimmers into galas/meets.

Supine Position: A horizontal face-up head, body and leg position.

Sweep: A phase of the propulsive elements in an arm stroke, leg kick or sculling action.

Swim Bench: A resistance training bench, use as a part of land training, with weights and pulleys, specially designed to mimic the stroke actions in the water.

Swim-Down: see Warm-Down

Swimming Log see Logbook

Swim-off: In a heat/finals type competition, a race after the scheduled event to break a tie.

Synchronised Swimming: A combination of swimming, dance and gymnastics, performed to music, competing either in solo or team events.

T

Taper: The resting process in training for swimming competition. As a major competition draws near, the swimmer will "taper" off the distances swum, to enable the swimmer to compete at their peak capability during the competition.

Target Time: The time given for a swimmer to complete a set or rep, which usually includes the rest interval.

Teaching Pool: A pool, usually shallow or with an adjustable depth, that is specifically used for teaching. Sometimes used as a competition cool-down pool.

Test Sets: Training sets where the results are recorded to monitor a variety of criteria including the swimmer's fitness and/or the effectiveness of the training programme.

Threshold Set: A high-intensity training set, to train the swimmer to raise their fitness 'threshold' at which they can tolerate larger amounts of lactic acid.

Time Graded Gala: A competition with qualifying times, which the swimmer must achieve before they can enter the event.

Time Trial: An event or series of events where a swimmer attempts to achieve a required qualifying time.

Timekeeper Timekeepers record the time for competitors swimming in their lane. The chief timekeeper collects the times from the timekeepers and reviews them with the referee.

Touchpad: The removable plate (at the end of the pool) that is connected to an electronic timing system. A swimmer must properly touch the touchpad to register an official time in a race.

Track Start: A start where the swimmer places their feet one in front of the other on the blocks.

Training Camp: There are many types of training camps for just about every level of swimmer, usually organised by the club, county, regional/state or national association.

Training Overload: A type of training which overloads the swimmer with a series of intense training sets. The aim is that the swimmer adapts to this type of training and becomes fitter and stronger as a result.

Training Plan: see Lesson Plan

Training Set: A block of work during training, usually containing several reps and focusing on one type of training activity.

Training Systems: There are two main training systems. Aerobic: A system that requires oxygen and Anaerobic: A system that doesn't require oxygen.

Training Zones: The different types of swimming training i.e. anaerobic, aerobic, sprint etc.

Transition Turns: The turns in an individual medley that transfers the swimmer from one stroke to another.

Transition: see Breakout

Transitions (Triathlon): The period of a race where the triathlete transfers from one discipline to another. Either from the swim to the bike or the bike to the run.

Triathlon: A competitive event which comprises of three continuous phases, a swim, a bike ride and a run. Distances for each phase can vary.

TT: see Time Trial

Tucked: The position a swimmer should adopt when performing a tumble turn. Chin on the chest, knees on stomach and heels on bottom.

Tumble Turn: The competitive freestyle or backstroke turn, sometimes referred to as the flip turn.

Turn Flags: see Backstroke Turn Flags

U

U/W: An abbreviation for underwater

Underwater Dolphin Kick: Performed by the swimmer in a tight streamlined position, with a vigorous double legged kick from below the knees. Commonly used during starts and turns for all strokes.

Undulation: The wave-like motion with the body a swimmer performs while swimming butterfly.

Unilateral Breathing: Breathing to one side while swimming freestyle. This can lead to an imbalance in the stroke over time. (see bilateral breathing)

Upsweep: see Sweep

V

VO2 Max: Distance training sets where swimmers are asked to swim as close to their maximum oxygen uptake will allow.

W

Warm-Down: see Cooldown.

A series of pool and poolside activities used by the swimmer after training or competition, essential for a swimmer's recovery and important for avoiding.

Warm-Down Pool: see Cooldown pool.

Warm-Up: A series of pool and poolside activities used by the swimmer before training or competition. Essential to warm-up the muscles and stimulate the blood flow.

Weekly Training Plan: Produced by the coach and is an outlined plan of the week's training session.

Weight Training: Traditionally performed by senior swimmers, using free weights, but is increasingly performed using pulleys and levers, swimmers perform a series of weight resistant exercises to increase strength and power during their land training programme.

Whipping Area: A room or area used during competition, on or near the poolside/deck, where the swimmers assemble before their event.

Y

Year Age: Age-determined events are categorised by the age of a swimmer on a specific date, usually either at year-end or the date of the competition.

Youth Swimmers: Swimmers usually aged 14 -17 years for girls and 15 – 18 for boys.